To David & Bernie,

Thanks so much for
supporting my efforts to
help build a primary school
in Africa —and inspiring me
on my climb up Kilimanjaro.

Love,
Sara
December 2012

THE
MOUNTAIN WITHIN

At the summit (left to right). Back row: Hans von Stiegel, Herta von Stiegel, Kyle Portbury, Chris Parsons, Alexander Adams, Elloy (the guide), John Hauf. Front row: Bryan Magee, Susie Snudden, Luke Purse. *(Photograph courtesy of Susie Snudden)*

THE
MOUNTAIN
WITHIN

LEADERSHIP LESSONS
and
INSPIRATION *for*
YOUR CLIMB TO THE TOP

HERTA VON STIEGEL
WITH GINA SMITH

NEW YORK   CHICAGO   SAN FRANCISCO
LISBON   LONDON   MADRID   MEXICO CITY   MILAN
NEW DELHI   SAN JUAN   SEOUL   SINGAPORE
SYDNEY   TORONTO

The **McGraw·Hill** Companies

Copyright © 2011 by Herta von Stiegel. All rights reserved. Printed in the United States of America. Except as permitted under the United States Copyright Act of 1976, no part of this publication may be reproduced or distributed in any form or by any means, or stored in a database or retrieval system, without the prior written permission of the publisher.

1 2 3 4 5 6 7 8 9 10   DOC/DOC   1 6 5 4 3 2 1

MHID   0-07-177306-1
ISBN 978-0-07-177306-5

e-book MHID   0-07-177325-8
e-book ISBN 978-0-07-177325-6

Design by Mauna Eichner and Lee Fukui
Endpaper photographs are courtesy of Hans von Stiegel.

McGraw-Hill books are available at special quantity discounts to use as premiums and sales promotions or for use in corporate training programs. To contact a representative, please e-mail us at bulksales@mcgraw-hill.com.

This book is printed on acid-free paper.

To the most important men and women in my life:

my parents, Georg and Johanna Ludwig,
for giving me life,

my parents-in-law, Jack and Ruth von Stiegel,
for accepting me into their family,

my sister, Hilde Weber,
whose perseverance changed my world,

my nephew, Daniel Weber,
for being a son and a friend,

my husband, Hans von Stiegel,
whose unconditional love gives me wings and whose
caution keeps my feet firmly planted on the ground

CONTENTS

PREFACE

THIS BOOK IS ABOUT LEADERSHIP, because we need a new brand of business and political leaders who know who they are. We need leaders who can relate spiritually and humanely to their fellow human beings, who can overcome challenges and exhibit innovation, creativity, and the courage to tackle obstacles as they arise.

Although, in this case, it was an actual mountain that was scaled, leaders should realize that it is the mountain within that needs to be conquered, one day at a time. These leaders should use failures as stepping-stones for significance. They must be leaders who understand planning and pacing and the importance of creating winning teams and maintaining them. They must be leaders who know not to stay too long at the top, because the rarefied atmosphere in the upper echelons causes us to lose perspective, to become intoxicated with power, status, and wealth and to lose touch with what matters.

This book is a call to create a better, more sustainable framework based on integrity, transparency, good governance, the value of each human being, and the power of teamwork. Its message reinforces what all great leaders know: that we can accomplish so much more together than any one of us can accomplish separately.

In a story in which adventure meets practical business advice, this book follows two narratives about climbing mountains: one, a failure to reach the summit of Mount Kilimanjaro, and the other, a successful mission to the top. The former, while painful in many ways, eventually served as the motivation and stepping-stone for the latter. What at first felt like a total failure ultimately formed a major part of the lessons outlined in this book.

The dramatic narrative of how I led a group of multinational and multi-ability people in my second attempt to reach the summit of Mount Kilimanjaro (Africa's highest mountain) is the main story line. Of a group of 28 climbers who started off, 16 members (almost 60 percent) of the group reached the top—a significantly better result than the usual statistic of 35 percent of climbers reaching the mountain's summit on expeditions. This turn of events is where I found the proof and inspiration that it's the people around us and our relationships with them that determine our level of success.

Each chapter tells a story about the leadership challenges that our team faced, both internally and externally, en route to reaching the summit of Mount Kilimanjaro. The narrative of climbing (and reclimbing) that great mountain is the foundation that I use to share powerful business and leadership lessons. These lessons are as applicable in the world of business as they are in a boulder-strewn field. Also, in each chapter, you'll find a conversation with one or two global business and political leaders who embody the lessons offered in that chapter. These individuals are among the world's most powerful and influential global leaders, representing the United States, Australia, Germany, the United Kingdom, Botswana, Kuwait, Egypt, Austria, South Korea, the Sudan, and Sweden.

Each of us has a mountain within to conquer on the way to the top, whether that top is a great physical feat or a goal of extraordinary career success. Each lesson is designed to be directly relevant to your climb in the corporate world, the political arena, or academia. The lessons shared in this book are also directly relevant to the global economic and political challenges we currently face and need to overcome.

It is my deepest desire to help you conquer your personal mountain and enable you to climb to the top without losing your soul. Now, let the journey begin.

ACKNOWLEDGMENTS

IT MAY TAKE A VILLAGE to raise a child, and it certainly takes the contribution of many people to complete a project of this magnitude, including two expeditions to the summit of Mount Kilimanjaro, the production of the documentary *The Mountain Within*, and the writing of this book .

I would like to acknowledge the following people, whose contributions played a significant role in the inspiration for and the writing of this book:

The multi-ability team of climbers, whose determination and trust made the Kilimanjaro expedition possible; Rodney Chamberlain, the chairman of Enham, whose vision and determination ensured that the project was not aborted prematurely; the board of trustees at Enham, who approved such a daring project, and the team that supported it; Maha al Juffali-Ghandour, the founder of the Help Center, who believes that every human being has value; our talented film crew, who captured the magic of the mountain and the release of human potential.

I would like to thank my friend Joanne Sawicki, who told me to write this book and who has been a constant source of encouragement throughout the entire process; my literary agent David C. Nelson, who recognized the value of my work and provided invaluable guidance; the 17 leaders profiled in this book, who have graciously shared their experiences and insights; and the visionary Gary Krebs and his highly professional team at McGraw-Hill, for making the writing of this book a most enjoyable experience for me,

I would also like to thank my talented coauthor Gina Smith and her organized husband, Henry, for their immense contribution to the manuscript.

And last, but certainly not least, I am eternally grateful to Hans, my husband and best friend, who listens to and often supports my crazy ideas, who encourages me when I want to give up, who puts my failures into perspective, and who celebrates my successes.

HERTA VON STIEGEL

I WOULD LIKE TO THANK my husband, Henry Schaefer, for his hard work on this project, my young son, Eric, for putting up with me during it, and Dr. Ruth Richards, my Ph.D. thesis chair. Special thanks to Herta for the invitation to this wonderful adventure and to the folks at Waterside, David C. Nelson in particular.

GINA SMITH

The
CLIMBERS

Alexander Adams, United Kingdom

Ahmed Afranji, Saudi Arabia

Steve Ballantyne, United Kingdom

Valerie Bradshaw, United Kingdom

James Bridges, United Kingdom

Gordon Brown, United States

Kate Coggins, United Kingdom

Elizabeth Curtis, United Kingdom

Pauline Griffin, United Kingdom

John Hauf, United States

Claire Holt, United Kingdom

Ali Jaafar, Saudi Arabia

Laura Jackson, United Kingdom

Jack Kreindler, United Kingdom

Bryan Magee, United Kingdom

Jamie Magee, United Kingdom

Eric Murphy, United States

Chris Parsons, United Kingdom

Kyle Portbury, Australia

Michael Price, United Kingdom

Luke Purse, United Kingdom

Sheila Ridge, United Kingdom

Gregory Rinaldi, Canada

Morgan Roy, Australia

James Smith, United Kingdom

Susie Snudden, United Kingdom

Michael Steel, United Kingdom

Hans von Stiegel, United States/United Kingdom

Herta von Stiegel, United States/United Kingdom

The
MOUNTAIN
WITHIN

If you wish success in life,
make perseverance your bosom friend,
experience your wise counselor,
caution your elder brother
and hope your guardian genius.

—JOSEPH ADDISON
(1672–1719)
English essayist, poet, and politician

1

DESPAIR

IT WAS PITCH-BLACK that night on the rocky slopes of Mount Kilimanjaro. I was exhausted, scared, and grappling with one of the biggest decisions of my life: Should I leave the sick and ailing members of our climbing team behind and continue to the top? Or should I stop—or even reverse course?

It wasn't supposed to be like this. It was just the third day of our journey. The guides had told us that this would be an easy day, a respite from two previous days of hard climbing. But there I was, scrambling to find the torch in my rucksack, listening to the muffled curses of everyone else trying to find his. We were climbing over boulders at this point. How far away could camp be?

I was leading the group on this expedition, and what an unusual group it was: seven climbers from the United Kingdom and Saudi Arabia with a variety of physical and mental disabilities, supported by their nondisabled "buddies." I'd brought them here on a philanthropic mission—to stretch the limits of what they thought they could do. It was the first

1

expedition by a truly multinational, multi-ability team to attempt to reach the summit of Mount Kilimanjaro.

I was prepared. If anything, I was overprepared. But the long day's crawl over unforgiving rock and shale had taken its toll that evening. I saw people starting to give up, to turn back. One of them, Val Bradshaw, began to vomit.

"She'll have to go back, Herta," one of our two mountain medics, Jack, told me. Severe mountain sickness can strike even the most experienced climbers without warning and randomly. It begins with a headache and disorientation. Left untreated, cerebral swelling sets in, often with fatal results.

It required extra effort for me to nod reluctantly. We'd been climbing for three days. I knew that Val didn't want to give up, but I realized that she had to. She was just too sick. But can a leader keep going when some of her team members cannot? It seemed wrong. At the same time, it also seemed necessary that I continue, no matter what. The mountain was a struggle, to be sure. But it was also merely one component of a greater personal struggle that I couldn't just shrug off.

There is a point on every difficult journey when you question your own abilities. On this particular journey, I was sure that I had the right planning, the right leadership, and the right set of skills. However, 25 years of scaling my way up the corporate ladder had taught me that nothing is ever as easy as you think it will be. Even with that in mind, I had never expected things to get so rough this early in the trip.

Several members of my team had already turned back by the third day. What were the odds, I wondered, of our ever reaching the summit at that rate? Should I even bother continuing? Few on this expedition knew that I had tried to conquer this mountain once before and failed, an experience that is discussed in detail in later chapters. The outcome of that previous attempt haunted me on the present one. It was against everything I believe in to try again and fail again.

As for Val, we needed to move on and leave her behind. The medics tried to make her comfortable, although her staying behind, apart from the group, was also dangerous. People warned me about how foolhardy and risky this mission was. As we continued ahead, the receding view of Val with our two mountain medics hovering over her really hammered the risks home.

Failure, or rather the fear of failure, filled my head like a familiar rhyme, impossible to shake off. I knew that feeling, growing up as I did as an ethnic German in Communist Romania. Back then, it had been up to me to help my family join my sister as émigrés to the United States. Terrified of the secret police—who could make anyone disappear with a flick of a finger—I experienced firsthand what truly high stakes felt like. Standing in line facing questions from such fearsome authorities prepared me well for the work I would later do at companies like Citibank, JPMorgan, and AIG. Staring into the faces of business leaders who had that same cool arrogance, I could always tell myself that they didn't have the power that those secret police did, a power that meant that one wrong word when they were questioning me could mean a jail sentence or certain death. Once I had faced them, I found that there was little in the corporate world that could frighten me.

But now I was up against a faceless, darkened mountain—not a room full of corporate executives. Unlike in my dealings in the corporate world, here there was no room for negotiation, no use in putting on a tough façade.

Fighting my way across the sharp shale of Mount Kilimanjaro, I told myself that the courage I'd gained in my childhood could somehow help, even here. I knew that the lives of these people could depend on the decisions I made. I knew that some of our party were unhappy about the way the expedition was going. They were even muttering among themselves about being insufficiently briefed on the possibility of having to leave halfway up the mountain and go back down without being given a fair chance to reach the summit. I was deflated and angry. I even began to question my own abilities.

"Can you sing, Herta?" asked one of the women in our group, Claire Holt. Her voice rang out, startling me out of my fearful inner state. "Know any hymns?"

Yes, I had learned how to sing from my Seventh-Day Adventist upbringing behind the Iron Curtain. I also knew the words to many a hymn. Together, Claire and I struck up a spirited chorus as we continued to climb up through the darkness.

Worry set in again, of course. If it was going to be a disaster, it would be my fault. It would mean that I had let these brave people down.

Our singing lapsed into silence. All I could hear was the scraping of our boots on the rough ground and my own labored breathing. Everyone was fighting a battle. Here was my group—these people that I'd brought up here to push themselves physically and emotionally—and now they were at extremes that they'd never faced before. I knew that even some of those who reached camp that day would be forced to go down the next day. The expedition leaders and the doctors would have to decide who was physically able to go on and tackle the summit, and who would have to go back down the mountain. For those who had put their all into coming this far, it would be a crushing blow.

There was a light ahead. We were at last approaching camp. As I stumbled toward the tents, Ali Jaafar, one of the Saudi climbers, came out to help me. "Thank God you made it," he said. His hands slipped under the straps of my rucksack and took the weight. "Here, let me carry this for you."

I had been fighting despair for so long that this simple gesture of kindness was too much. I began to weep. I couldn't help it. I was so physically exhausted that all my emotional defenses began to erode. Even though it was against what I perceived to be my identity—the expedition leader, the tough businesswoman—at that moment, I simply sat down and cried.

The painful trek through the boulder field, the sick climbers I was responsible for, and the very real possibility that this expedition would turn out to be a colossal failure (again!) had become overwhelming. My thoughts grew even darker as the night progressed. Self-doubts engulfed me, as if my first failure on this mountain was the real truth: I was incapable of accomplishing this goal. It was my doubts that threatened to undermine our chances of success this time around.

Was it against everyone's interest to keep going and keep believing? Was I being arrogant—even selfish—by continuing to hope for success? With the future of the expedition uncertain, I allowed myself to sink into despair.

LEADERSHIP LESSON NO. 1: RESILIENCE

In business and in our personal lives, we all have our dark moments of despair. These are existential moments, the "dark night of the soul" that medieval mystics spoke so eloquently about.

Closing a deal or taking something to the next step—especially when you're fresh from a painful failure—is difficult. It's easy to keep going when things look positive and are going your way. It's a different story altogether when you are in the dark and there is no obvious means of escape. It is there, in those dark moments, that the choice must be made either to persevere or to give up. A conscious decision to persevere is required. As concentration camp survivor and great existentialist thinker Viktor Frankl pointed out, your attitude, in the end, is the one thing that is always within your control.

When the situation looks dark—when success seems remote—there is no better time to choose an attitude of persistence, an attitude of *resilience*. This, I have seen, is the key to keeping going when despair threatens to hold you back from the success that is almost within your grasp.

Resilience is a concept that has been around for centuries. The idea of bouncing back from adversity, being able to survive and even thrive despite trauma or even a series of traumas, is at least as old as Confucius. "Our greatest glory is

CHOOSE TO PERSEVERE

Whenever the outlook starts to look grim, persevere; don't give up. Persevere when things are tough and you can't even see the light at the end of the tunnel. Don't give up, no matter what. Persevere, whether you are struggling across a boulder field or in a conference room, whether you are dealing with the secret police or with hostile executives who can destroy your career, even when (or especially when) you don't have a penny to your name. Look inward and remember your high points, those moments of undeniable success that you've achieved. Look to your personal life also for the resources and guidance that you need—it's not all about business. Remember that calm voice from inside that brought clarity to chaotic times in the past. Remember those moments when the stakes were high and you made it work. Perseverance is what gets us through, and it is the first step toward bouncing back, brushing oneself off, and resuming one's course.

not in never failing," the Chinese philosopher said. "Rather it is in rising every time we fall."

The best psychological researchers in the world have examined resilience as a rare but very real character trait appearing among certain victims of trauma, turmoil, torture, and tragedy. Researchers are perennially looking for answers to why this is the case. Why do some survivors emerge from their terrible experiences unshaken, or even stronger? As answers have bubbled to the top, a set of traits that match so-called resilients is emerging. It is fair to say that people are unlikely to rise to the top without a surplus of resilience. It is a quality that you must cultivate, but rest assured that you can learn to become more resilient even if you weren't born that way. Researchers the world over, including Emmy Werner, with her renowned four-decade study of impoverished Hawaiian children, have identified these traits of resilient people:

- *An attitude of perseverance.* Resilient people don't give up. They use positive self-talk to keep themselves upbeat in the face of the worst possible outcomes.

- *Self-reinvention.* Resilient people are also found to have an enormous capacity for reinventing themselves in new roles after a major trauma or failure. They have incredible plasticity in this regard. What better way to bounce back than by adjusting and adapting?

- *Courage.* In business or on the mountain, resilient survivors tend to look at the events of their lives less personally, taking their failures, no matter how painful, as life lessons that they can build upon.

- *Reliance on a mentor.* Studies show that the resilient among us have someone to lean on, check in with, and gain perspective from. Sometimes the best way to get through troubled times is by speaking with someone who's been there before.

- *Restorable self-esteem.* It sounds obvious, but the ability to hold one's unique beliefs and outlook as utterly distinct from what one accomplishes is a key factor in resilience. The people who bounce back best are those who decide that circumstances have failed them, not the other way around.

Nancy Palmer, one of the leading U.S. researchers on resilience, says that the phenomenon is so complex, it is almost impossible to take apart. Says Palmer: "It takes personal characteristics such as social skills and environmental factors to create the resilience phenomenon. Resilience does not just come from the person. Additionally, it draws on biological and psychological characteristics of the person. The environment's role cannot be forgotten . . . people, opportunities, and atmospheres all add to the resilience equation."

Success in the face of adversity takes a commitment to becoming resilient—and it's not easy. "Great sacrifice is made and pain is endured for a person to display resilience," says Palmer. "Resilient people face tremendous stress and adversity."

No matter how difficult, though, one thing is certain to anyone who has survived enormous adversity and managed to succeed and even thrive: success is dependent on resilience, on the choice to persevere.

▶ *In conversation with* ◀
KAY UNGER

Kay Unger embodies persistent resilience. I met the famed designer when we were both in Chicago attending a board meeting of the Committee of 200 (C200), an organization of preeminent businesswomen. I had just arrived at the hotel and was making contingency plans, since my luggage had somehow taken a detour. "What should I wear?" I wondered aloud. One of my fellow C200 members said, "You need to talk to Kay. She'll fix you up."

I knew that Kay was a wonderful designer whose clothes are sold under the Kay Unger New York and Phoebe Couture labels and have been worn by celebrities like Oprah Winfrey, Salma Hayek, and Tyra Banks. Her designs have been featured on television programs, including *Gossip Girl*, *The Sopranos*, and *Sex and the City*. At first glance, Kay seemed to be another successful entrepreneur—someone I admired for making it to the top of her profession without ever losing her grounding. But once I got to know her, I realized that none of it had come easily.

As a young woman, all Kay had ever wanted to do was design beautiful clothing. She used a legacy of $25,000 from her father, a successful investment banker who died young, to set up her own company. Knowing nothing about business, she brought in two partners to help her. By the end of the 1980s, the company was a multimillion-dollar operation. In her personal life, she'd achieved success as well; she was married with two healthy children. Everything seemed to be going her way.

Gradually, though, Kay began to feel in her gut that something wasn't right. She'd always kept to the design side of things, leaving the business and operational focus of the company to her partners. Despite all the surface success of this arrangement, something seemed off, although she couldn't place what it was.

Suddenly, one of her two partners left the company after a bitter argument with the other. The remaining partner seemed to be enjoying a far more lavish lifestyle than Kay herself felt she could afford. Her personal accountant suggested that money was bleeding from the company, but that was all the accountant could see.

Money troubles worsened, and finally Kay and her partner lost control of the company. It was forced into bankruptcy. Worse still, years before this occurred, Kay's partners and the company's lawyer had asked her to sign personal guarantees for millions of dollars. That meant that not only had she lost her business, but the corporate veil had been pierced. As a result of embezzlement by a partner, she faced personal ruin.

"My partner walked away from the ruins relatively unscathed, but I was being sued for $7 million. Luckily—or so I thought—at the time I signed the guarantees, my accountant had persuaded me to put some of my assets, including the family home, into my husband's name, to safeguard them. At least, I thought, my children will have a roof over their heads."

It was at this point that her husband announced that he was leaving her. Kay had lost every single thing she owned and loved. She didn't have so much as a credit card to her name.

"But I kept remembering my father's words," she said. "He died before I really had time to learn about business from him. But I do remember that, while I was still in school, he told me: 'Kay, if you've never seen the bottom and worked your way back up from that horrible place, you will never know what it is really like to feel successful and free.'"

Kay went on to tell me about the lowest moment in her life. "I had lost everything I owned," Kay said. "A few months before I had been worth millions, or so I thought—but now I found myself walking home 30 blocks through New York because I had no money for a cab." This long walk seemed to Kay a dark preview of things to come. "That was the day when, plodding home without carfare, I hit bottom," she told me. "I had lost not only all my money but my good name—I had called the company Kay Unger, and now that company had gone bust. It appeared to the world as if I had caused the failure and was responsible to the creditors. The worst thing was to feel so out of control. I had always been determined to be self-sufficient and not rely on a man to support me, yet now I had nothing."

Yet even after staring down the prospect of losing it all, Kay managed to bounce back. She refused to give up hope even under these seemingly hopeless circumstances. She had two teenage children to support, and she was determined that she would fight her way out of failure and back to the top.

Her saving grace was that she was well known and liked in the business and had never compromised her ethical standards. Out of the blue, or so it seemed, one of her former employees came to her with an offer from an Asian factory owner and a rescue proposition. Kay decided to start over and rebuild her business from scratch.

First she renegotiated a lease on one of the offices that the company had relinquished. Then her children helped her repaint it and turn it into a showroom. With just a skeleton crew, Kay began a new business. Today, Kay heads Phoebe Couture, her own small but highly respected company, with revenues of about $40 million and a leaner, fitter core staff of 50 employees. She continues to draw accolades from the fashion industry and from the clients who wear her beautiful designs. However, because of her experience, Kay is now a balanced and centered person who enjoys her rewards.

"I will never forget how bad I felt that day, walking home, with not a cent to my name and with my reputation in tatters," she said. "But my father was right. If you've never been bankrupt and learned from it, how can you ever really understand and appreciate the rewards of success?"

2

The CALLING

WHY ARE SOME OF US driven to achieve our visions of success and not just dream them? High achievers in many different fields—business, politics, the arts—have often told me what my own experience confirms: that it goes all the way back to childhood. Most go-getters say that, to them, success feels like a calling. Achieving one's vision can be painful, difficult work at times, but those who have actually done so claim that they had no choice but to do it.

Maybe that explains why I found myself in the middle of a crisis that night I described in the previous chapter, halfway up dark and dangerous Mount Kilimanjaro with the group I was leading. Maybe that explains why I was sitting there, in pain and in doubt, instead of confidently walking in my designer pumps to conquer the mountain in the same way I would close another multimillion-dollar business deal. In the corporate world, I would know just what to do, but here I was out of my comfort zone.

That night in 2008, after stumbling across the boulder field and arriving at camp with fewer climbers than I had started with, I was still unsure whether we'd make it. But I had no intention of giving up. I simply refused. This calling I had—to take this group up the mountain—had been born many years before, and I'd scrupulously planned for the difficult moments I was experiencing now.

The first time I laid eyes on Mount Kilimanjaro was in 1995. I was on safari with Hans, my husband, and I was awed by the beautiful snow-covered peak that suddenly seemed to rocket before me. It glistened and twinkled. I was mesmerized. I turned to Hans. "I want to climb that," I told him. He looked at me with those large brown eyes of his as if I had two heads.

I didn't lose that sense of awe, though. On returning to London, I kept feeling that, yes, it *was* my destiny to scale that mountain. I knew it would be tough, even painful, but I would do it. With the same spirit that I regularly employed when doing battle in the boardroom, I was going to conquer that beautiful snow-capped mountain.

I was always this way. Growing up in the harsh light of Communist Romania was a grim beginning to my life, even though my religious parents loved me and did everything they could to give me the best possible start. It was a time of poverty and fear for us. We suspected a teenage neighbor of being an informant. Our mail always arrived ripped at the seams; the secret police didn't even bother to be secretive about it. It felt as if they knew what we were having for breakfast. If we hadn't found a way to leave in the mid-1970s, I can't imagine where I would be now. We were very fortunate to escape.

For me, academic achievement was a possible way out of our difficulties. I was a serious student who never fell behind in my studies, even if it meant studying after working in the vineyards with my family just to survive. Some early mornings, I'd ask my mother to wake me up at 5 a.m. so that I could complete my academic work to my own highest standards. I'd plunge my feet in cold water to keep awake, if that was what it took. Incredibly, despite my consistently high marks in school, the institution eventually expelled me because my religious beliefs did not allow me to go to school on Saturdays with the rest of the class.

Scaling the heights of adversity and fighting failure as we went along was a way of life for us under the Communist regime. Even acquiring the barest necessities took enormous care and determination in that bleak, monochromatic world. One year, when other regions in the country had food shortages, the government established a bartering system for buying such basic items as oil and sugar. My family was no exception when this system was implemented; one day my mother entrusted me with two eggs to take to the store in exchange for a bit of oil. The eggs were only the ticket to the transaction, though; we still had to pay for the oil with cash.

That day, knowing that the lines would be long and supplies would be limited, I woke up at 3 a.m. to get a place in line before the store opened at 7 a.m. As the opening time neared, the crowd started pressing and jostling—so much so that I fainted. When I came to, the eggs were still in my possession. Some kind soul must have supported me and also fetched some water, because somehow the eggs remained unbroken. I handed them over when my time came and returned home triumphant with that half-liter of oil. It was a victory.

Climbing Mount Kilimanjaro? Compared with surviving and escaping from Romania, that would be easy. Or so I thought in 1995 as I set for myself the deceptively simple goal of conquering the mountain for my fortieth birthday.

Of course, it wasn't so simple. Identifying a vision and realizing that you have a calling are just the initial steps of a long journey. Naïve as I was back then about mountains, even I recognized that I would need to be fully prepared. And getting fit was another part of getting started. Remember, I grew up among the mountainous landscape of Transylvania, which is nowhere near as stony and lifeless as the Dracula legends portray it. In Transylvania, the foothills are lined with orchards and rolling vineyards. Above, in the high mountains, there are spectacular vistas. I had walked in the hills as a child and had loved them ever since. There is nothing quite like that sense of accomplishment when you've made it above the valley, able to see the world spread out at your feet.

Mount Kilimanjaro, though—that was altogether different. This mountain has a high peak of some 6,000 meters, and I had never been particularly athletic. All my previous goals through childhood and my career in finance had been intellectual ones. Now, the weight of a dramatic physical goal started to reach obsessive proportions. Despite long days in the office and dark, rainy nights, I tried to go to the gym almost every night for at least an hour, no matter how weary I was.

Hans kept me focused. Once he saw how serious I was, he threw himself into the adventure, too. He became my partner in going to the gym, letter writing, and research—basically everything it took to compare the alternatives and decide on the right expedition and guides for the Kilimanjaro goal. We wanted an experienced firm that exuded safety and professionalism, and the one we finally settled on seemed to fit the bill. The company mapped out a trip that would train us: a climb up a smaller mountain, Mount Meru, to aid us in getting acclimated to the altitude, the temperatures, and the general environment of the experience before we attacked the terrifying and thrilling adventure that would be Kilimanjaro.

I approached this project the way I approached any business project: breaking the process down into a series of smaller steps. As I started checking items off the list, I remained ever vigilant, never taking my eye off the ball. I had a calling. I had a vision. Now I just had to see it through to completion.

There were doubts, of course. Would I be in good enough shape? Had we done enough thorough research? As usual, Hans had the answers I needed, the ones I instinctively knew inside: "Everything you put your mind to is a success, darling—and for goodness' sake, it is only a mountain."

His words comforted me at the time. It *was* only a mountain. But later, lying on that mountain on a cold October night and reflecting on all this, I saw that nothing in my life had ever been just a mountain.

LEADERSHIP LESSON NO. 2:
CAREER VS. CALLING

What is your calling? Knowing deep inside that you have a specific calling for a vocation, an achievement in life, is something that is difficult to ignore. Ignoring it means frustration. The writer and philosopher Joseph Campbell referred to heeding a calling as "following your bliss." Doing so leads to a deep sense of satisfaction and meaning in your life. The American author Frederick Buechner defines it as "that place where our deep gladness meets the world's deep need." Centuries earlier, Confucius advised his followers, "Choose a job you love, and you will never have to work a day in your life." This is timeless advice that still applies today.

Psychologists have delved deeply into the idea of having a calling and to where it comes from. Some define it as having a transcendent feeling—that is, literally feeling that you have been called to your vocation. It is an inspiration that grabs hold of you and leads you where you are meant to go. A calling is not a goal that we create and control. Instead, it is a teacher that we listen to and follow if we have the courage and the desire to reach our highest aspirations.

A calling might also be considered to be a sudden realization that can come at any point in life, letting you know that, yes, this vocation or goal will bring ultimate value to your existence. Whether it's something that you felt from an early age or something that came later, though, following your calling brings meaning to your life. Someone with a calling loves what he does and is willing to go to any lengths to continue pursuing it.

We all know what our calling is. We know it by remembering what we wanted to be when we were children, how we envisioned our careers when we began them, and even what types of books we read and leisure activities we enjoyed.

HANG ON TO YOUR VISION

People will discourage you. They may tell you that your vision of how you see your success is unrealistic, culturally wrong, unsophisticated, or impractical. But if you have a vision in your heart (if you feel it), you know it. Choose to do more than just build a career, important as that may be. Discover your calling, your passion, and pursue your vision, not just for money or fame but to make a difference in the world.

As a child, I wanted to be a lawyer when I grew up. This wasn't a career goal that I inherited, at least not in the conventional sense. My parents, although both of them were highly intelligent, had had only an eighth-grade education. The brutality of World War II and the Communist regime that followed had severely limited their academic advancement. Ironically, the inspiration for my desire to become a lawyer came from my mother's experience during the war. My mother and grandmother were court-martialed because of their religious beliefs and sentenced to 25 years in prison. Their sentence was commuted, in part because of the eloquent defense of skilled lawyers. As a result, I thought lawyers were fantastic, and, given that I was very articulate even as a small child, I wanted to grow up and help people by being a successful lawyer. In due time, I became one. When I moved from law into business, the desire to make a difference in people's lives was still deeply ingrained in my mind.

If you are not already working in a position that is aligned with your calling, I advise you to give your choice of work a long, hard look. Overall, executives who are working within their calling report better success at work, more comfort with the decisions they make, a clear view of their life path, and a deep commitment to what they do day-to-day. Every action counts to a person with a calling.

Executives who say that they have a calling also report less job stress, longer tenure, more career satisfaction, and higher salaries overall. They feel that their lives have a deeper meaning. While it is paramount to acquire all the skills, education, and experience necessary for a fruitful career, it is not enough. A calling transcends the most successful career. It is much more than the size of your bank accounts, another accolade, a title, or a promotion. A calling encompasses all the satisfaction and excitement you feel as you move through life.

It is never too late to discover your calling or to begin to follow it again if you feel you have lost it. Imagine yourself as an eyewitness to your own funeral. Try to visualize the people in your life and imagine what you would want them to tell others about what you brought to the world through your career and your leadership choices. Are you building the life that you were meant to create?

The work you do can be a gift to the world. If you feel that your career is falling short of your own personal calling, not only are you robbing the world of your own particular gift, but you are robbing yourself of the deep self-satisfaction and meaning that come from knowing that you are doing what you feel you are meant to be doing. You need to follow your calling if you are to ultimately succeed.

▶ *In conversation with* ◀
SUNG-JOO KIM

If there ever was a poster child for this second leadership lesson, it would be my friend Sung-Joo Kim. Recently named one of the "top 50 women in the world to watch" by the *Wall Street Journal* and one of the "seven most powerful women in Asia" by *AsiaWeek*, the tall, elegant, soft-spoken Sung-Joo is a force to be reckoned with.

Throughout her climb to the top, Sung-Joo had a hard and firm grasp on what she wanted to do—a true vision. A woman of deep faith, she hung on to that vision with such tenacity that not even the worst troubles and criticisms could deflate her.

Sung-Joo is the founder of a retail group, the Sung-joo Group, which runs dozens of franchise retail stores in South Korea, including Gucci, Yves Saint Laurent, and Marks & Spencer. Additionally, she is the CEO and chair of MCM group, a Germany-based luxury products company. MCM purses and bags can be seen on the arms of the world's richest celebrities now, but it wasn't always so. Sung-Joo acquired the company when it was ailing, turned it around, and made it into a $400 million global phenomenon by focusing on customer service, practical designs, and cost-effective production. Born in South Korea to a wealthy business family, Sung-Joo was discouraged from working at all after college. Her father finally disowned her for her rebellious idea of choosing her own boyfriend rather than entering into an arranged marriage. But Sung-Joo was determined to follow her calling. She started from scratch, and she never lost sight of the path she had laid out for herself.

Sung-Joo wanted to prove that even in a patriarchal country such as Korea, a woman could rise to the top. She wanted to show that a woman or a man could do so without compromising honesty or transparency. This vision has made Sung-Joo one of the most respected businesspeople—male or female—in all of Asia. And lastly, she wanted to prove that it was possible to start a small company or run a medium-size company and grow it to gigantic, global proportions.

"I never really tried to strive for money or fame," Sung-Joo told me, explaining that she actually had had three interwoven visions as she climbed up her ladder of success. "First of all, because I was a woman, my duties were only going to the right college and having an arranged marriage," she said. But Sung-Joo wanted more out of life, and she wanted it on her own terms.

"My mission also included fighting against corruption," she told me, explaining that, when she was building her business from scratch, she was expected and encouraged to take and give bribes to make things easier and get things done. "Corruption comes in very easily. At the beginning, I faced enormous resistance for not accepting bribes or giving kickbacks to buyers. But I wanted to prove that with a clean hand, without corruption, you could win."

"I also tried to educate my team on that," she added. "Because we don't rely on anything like bribes or kickbacks, we have to prove that we have force in our strategies and that we respect ourselves in the way we treat others and consumers. It was clearly proven that, during the Asian financial crisis of 1998, more than 40,000 small to medium-size companies went bankrupt. But we survived." It showed, she told me, that practicing honestly (her mission from the beginning) was not just *a* way to success; it was *the* way.

"Transparency and clean policy is true competitiveness— and we've proven so," she told me. During the financial crisis, she lost $30 million overnight, but she was determined to do everything in her power to save her company, including selling its crown jewel, the Gucci franchise. She sold it for $27 million, much more than the buyer thought a fire sale would command, but she was determined to do it with clean and honest books. The buyers respected her so much for her approach and became so convinced of the value of the franchise that they paid the asking price.

"Transparency gives you strength," she told me, her face shining as she explained her philosophy. She told me that she is driven by a strong faith in God and the assurance that she is not just building a career, but following her calling. I could plainly see her satisfaction from the fact that she had hung on so dearly to her mission of being a woman in business in Asia—a woman who can run her business honestly and without bribes, and can take major companies to the global market, even when she has to start from scratch. Sung-Joo is a lesson to us all.

3

The
FIRST ATTEMPT

BEFORE KILIMANJARO came Mount Meru. Just 70 kilometers from Kili, Meru's 4,600-meter height made it a good practice mountain, or so our guides suggested. We were to scale Mount Meru, descend it, rest for a day, and only then begin to conquer Kilimanjaro—the mountain we'd set our true sights on.

The morning we began our ascent of Meru was a steamy subtropical day teeming with insects. Entrenched in that unique African mix of wild beauty and terrible danger, I felt the first taste of fear. I looked around at the retinue accompanying us for this trial expedition. Aside from Hans and me, there were about 10 other climbers, the laden porters, and the guides. One of the nature reserve guides flanking our little party, Michael, was carrying a gun. So were his companions. I watched him take in every inch of the jungle trail in front of us and around us. He caught my eye and nodded toward my feet.

"Elephant," he said.

I saw then that we were stepping over giant, steaming piles of dung. Elephant dung. I'd seen elephants before, though only safely from the back of a Land Rover. Peering nervously into the undergrowth, I realized that this elephant—or its whole family, judging from the sheer amount of dung on the trail—could come crashing out at any second. They could be only a few meters away, and I wouldn't see them until they were right upon us.

Michael smiled at my nervousness. "They use this trail at night."

So had I only imagined the freshness of the dung? Was the heat of the morning sun responsible for the steam I noticed? Either way, it was a fresh reminder. I was out of the world where a business card or title mattered at all. Here, the world and its animals played by different rules.

This was what I'd come for, I realized then, as my fear gave way to joy at the utter freedom that the expedition afforded. I was here to experience nature, to see what I was really made of, and to face a very different kind of challenge from anything I'd experienced before. The beautiful surroundings reminded me how much more there is to the world than money and business and climbing the corporate ladder. No one cared about my title or my bonus on this mountain. That wasn't what life was supposed to be about. At the end of the night, sitting around a campfire in front of the tents we pitched, I saw what it was truly all about: community, companionship, and resourcefulness.

Over the next two days, as we climbed higher and higher up Meru, all of us new climbers began to experience the ill effects of altitude. The higher we climbed, the more difficult each step felt. My legs were leaden, and my breathing was ragged. After we climbed above the tree line, the air no longer seemed to satisfy my straining lungs. It was too thin and without enough oxygen. The guides kept urging us to drink, as dehydration could be a risk at these altitudes. The guides and porters, who climbed these peaks regularly, seemed so energetic compared to us. A headache hovered behind my eyes, and so did the return of my doubts. If this mountain was so difficult, I kept thinking, how would I fare on Kilimanjaro after just a day's rest? This kind of thinking led to failure, though, not success. Meru was a stepping-stone to something great—an experience that I would remember for the rest of my life—and I would not allow myself to weaken at this early stage.

I focused over and over on what Hans had said. I thought about the expedition as a business venture, breaking it down into doable chunks. Just as in business, where no one would finance your large venture before you'd proven your mettle on smaller projects, I had to prove myself on Meru. Failure was not an option, and it was in this way that I persevered, with the lure of the glittering goal of Kilimanjaro drawing me up the slopes of the smaller mountain.

Our final ascent took place in deep darkness. We could barely see our feet in front of us, and the terrain was uneven and unpredictable. I scrambled and stumbled, concentrating fiercely on my footing. Gradually, my tenuous belief that we would make it grew stronger as we neared Meru's peak. As the first light began rolling across the plains, we took our last few weary steps. We were tired, but exhilarated. We had made it to the top of Mount Meru—standing stock still on the surface, bathed by natural beauty and the exultation of this first victory. At the peak there was a holy silence, behind it just the faint whistle of wind and our own deep and tired breaths.

I could forget for a moment that scaling Meru was less than half of the real job done, because there, in front of me, from peak to peak, was the sunrise-haloed vista of Mount Kilimanjaro. I could do nothing but gaze silently at one peak from the vantage point of the other. Kilimanjaro took my breath away; it seemed to be a mountain floating on thick clouds. I'd never seen a more beautiful sight. The sense of destiny that I had felt when I originally saw Kili grew stronger at that moment. I knew then that I would achieve my dream.

"They call it the Rose Glow."

The guide's voice was weirdly slurred. He sounded almost drunk. I turned to him, reluctantly breaking away from the magnificent view of dawn over Kilimanjaro's snowy peak. The guide, Michael, gave me a lopsided grin. His legs seemed to buckle, and he caught hold of my arm for balance. "Sorry," he slurred. "Gotta sit down for a moment."

"Are you all right?" Suddenly our roles were reversed. Michael had steered me protectively up this first mountain, but now I found myself kneeling over his figure, slumped beside an outcrop of rock. His hands were chilly and blue. I tried to find his gloves in his pockets but could not, so I slipped off my gloves and forced them onto his hands. His eyes had closed, but he attempted clumsily to help me. I shrugged off my rucksack and began rummaging for extra clothes to wrap him in for warmth. He was fading in and out.

I understood what was happening. They had warned us about severe mountain sickness. It didn't matter that Michael climbed Meru at least once a week in the season; the illness can strike even the most experienced climbers without warning and seemingly at random. We had to get him down quickly, or he would die, and we had to move now. I shook his shoulder roughly.

"Michael! You can't sleep now!"

One of the other guides saw us and came to help us pull him to his feet. I took one last look at the fading Rose Glow radiating from the distant Kilimanjaro before we began our rapid descent from Meru's peak.

We dashed down the mountain at a breakneck pace. But a single thought gnawed at me from inside: if an experienced guide like Michael could succumb to altitude sickness so quickly and easily, what was in store for a novice like me?

LEADERSHIP LESSON NO. 3: PROJECT MANAGEMENT

How many times have you faced a deal or a goal that seemed overwhelming? The secret to successful project management is something that everyone already knows but keeps forgetting. You have to break big projects into smaller steps. The brain, scientists have discovered, handles complex tasks and memories by a technique they call "chunking." When you have a big project ahead of you, breaking it down into smaller, achievable parts is the surest path to success.

You are given a new project and a deadline. The project seems daunting, and completing it by the deadline seems impossible. You are overwhelmed. You might go to your friend or colleague and complain about how unreasonable the person who gave you this assignment is, and how you cannot possibly meet the deadline. Meanwhile, you are wasting time.

Spend the initial phase of a project analyzing its breadth and depth. Then break it down into achievable steps. That is how you finish your project on time without having to crash it at the end.

Authors especially know the power of this technique and have spoken widely on it. American author Mark Twain famously said, "The secret of getting ahead is getting started. The secret to getting started is breaking your complex overwhelming tasks into small manageable tasks, and then starting on the first one." Author John Steinbeck reached into the wrenching heart of the matter and wrote about the feeling when a large assignment looms. "When I face the desolate impossibility of writing 500 pages, a sick sense of failure falls on me, and I know I can never do it," Steinbeck said. "Then gradually, I write one page and then another. One day's work is all that I can permit myself to contemplate."

All big projects begin with little steps, and the way to start tackling the projects is by defining all those little steps. The power of your mind will then start to reduce your feelings of tension and distress as you begin to recognize that each step is manageable on its own. Your mentality changes as you become centered on finishing the initial smaller and more achievable steps.

As you finish one piece of the project puzzle, you are able to then go onto the next. The stress melts away, and the project no longer appears as overwhelming as it did earlier. I cannot even begin to describe how often I have felt stretched to the limit. I could offer a thousand examples from college, law school, and times in my career when I faced big challenges and had to break them down into manageable steps again and again. One of the more memorable challenges appeared in 1989, after I had joined Citibank in New York. The bank had serious difficulties at the time, and the stock price would eventually fall to $8 per share. Many of my colleagues expected the bank to go under and decided to cash in their stock options as soon as they were barely in the money. (In banking terms, that means selling shares as soon as there was a small profit.)

As the senior tax counsel for Europe, my contribution in turning the company around was to reduce Citicorp's draconian tax burden by more than $200 million. Obviously, this was a huge number, and it was by no means immediately clear how I would be able to reduce the tax burden by that amount. The task had to be done thoughtfully, within the confines of the laws and regulations of many jurisdictions and without damaging the reputation of the company. I had to tackle this goal one transaction at a time, with the support of my teams all over Europe.

One of the major deals that needed to be structured very carefully was the sale of the MesseTurm, an office building in Frankfurt. The pressure to finalize the deal, if possible, in a tax-efficient manner was enormous, but each one of us on the five-person core team did our part. We assumed that we would not have jobs by year-end if we did not conclude the transaction successfully, but that was not our primary concern. Instead, we did our very best, one day at a time, one aspect of the deal at a time, until we were able to execute the final documents just before Christmas 1990. The net proceeds from the transaction, it turned out, constituted more than 25 percent of Citicorp's global profits that year. To this day, when I visit Frankfurt and see the MesseTurm, I feel a sense of pride.

President Theodore Roosevelt once said, "I dream of men [and women] who take the next step instead of worrying about the next thousand steps." However, movement in itself is not enough. As an old Chinese proverb puts it, "It is better to take many small steps in the right direction than to make a great leap forward only to stumble backward."

As an executive, a manager, and a leader, not only should you make chunking a project into smaller steps a habit, but you should keep an eye out for employees who think that way, too, employees who, rather than becoming overwhelmed by a project, choose to tackle it with enthusiasm. They are the ones who will be the most successful—and, in turn, they will make you more successful.

In my experience, there are no shortcuts to success, no express elevators. Reaching the top comes one step at a time, one degree after another, one deal reinforcing the next. When success, perhaps in the form of a major promotion, seems sudden, when a major breakthrough occurs, it is generally founded on the discipline of accomplishing one chunk at a time.

So whenever you are faced with what seems like an overwhelmingly large project, ask yourself this question: "Can I take this project and divide it into smaller, more manageable

DIVIDE YOUR JOURNEY INTO STEPS

Your best chance at success in reaching a goal that you've set is to survey it in its entirety, then sit down and painstakingly divide it into small, achievable steps. Not only does this promote progress, but it reduces stress and gives you many small feelings of accomplishment along the way. And we all need as much self-encouragement as we can muster. As a side note, hire or train employees who are able to master this technique, too. This way, rather than being overwhelmed, they'll be optimistic and enthusiastic as they tick each small achievement off the list. These employees on your team will be the ones who are most likely to succeed, which in turn will make you and the whole team successful.

parts?" This is the question that makes a large and almost impossible project become feasible. It dissipates your fear and stress as you begin moving toward completion one step at a time. It will lead you to your most effective time and stress management strategies.

▶ *In conversation with* ◀

DR. JOACHIM FABER

Dr. Joachim Faber built Allianz Global Investors (AGI) into one of the biggest asset management firms in the world, managing more than $1.5 trillion. As its CEO, he brought AGI to where it is today from modest beginnings. He did so by making several transformational acquisitions, including Pimco, Nicholas Applegate, and RCM.

Joachim and I were colleagues at Citibank, where he was head of Capital Markets for Europe, North America, and Japan. Given his professional experience, I knew that he would be the perfect person with whom to discuss this leadership lesson—breaking down the journey or every major goal into a series of manageable steps.

In our conversation, he contrasted the whole of his career to other major projects. "My experience is that my career has been, if I'm totally honest, a wonderful series of very lucky circumstances where I was smart enough to decide quickly and determinedly to take opportunities as they arrived. During my career, I was probably also getting better at creating some of those opportunities rather than just waiting for them." The opportunities he spoke of—either arrived at or made—were enormous projects, he told me.

This is where "dividing the journey into steps" works best. Major goals and projects require "very intensive thinking about design and process. It is nothing other than dividing up certain goals and tasks into manageable and measurable steps." Of the eight major acquisitions that Joachim led, "all of them followed that same path, the same process."

Discipline played a big part in bringing major transactions to a successful conclusion. Joachim told me that he has never personally felt overwhelmed by a task: "First of all, I would say that if you feel overwhelmed by a project, don't take it. You are probably the wrong person for it, but I have rarely seen a goal that was not manageable. I can't say that I have ever declined a major project based on the fact that I didn't think it was manageable."

"But if you have taken the project on, then it is extremely important to be disciplined, to have a really well-thought-out plan. Work potentially long hours and have long meetings with people who know and who give instant input. At the beginning of a project, it is so important to develop the very precise and very detailed planning of that process, which then needs to be handled and managed with great discipline."

The immediate ability to see giant goals as achievable is a mindset that Joachim exemplifies. In addition to precise and detailed planning and the discipline to take large projects and turn them into reality, he feels very strongly that you have to take your team with you. This approach is most efficient and must permeate the entire organization. When he was making major acquisitions of German companies, for instance, human resource issues had to be handled with sensitivity, fairness, and discipline.

"In one case, we had made redundant about 600 people and in the second case about 400. I have, luckily, a very good head of human resources, and I said, 'You take your time. You are going to sit down with each individual person. You are going to find a good solution for each and every one of them, and if that takes six months, that's okay. If it takes nine months, it's okay. And if it takes twelve months, that's also okay."

The breakdown of this complex human resource matter to the individual level proved to be highly important and successful in various ways. As Joachim told it, "It was success-ful because we were able to give much more justice to the individual human situations. Second, we also got a much, much better economic result for the company."

Joachim always felt encouraged to approach what was given to him "as a series of tasks and just go for it with a lot of enthusiasm, a lot of spirit, and a lot of courage." He laughed good-naturedly at that last comment, wondering aloud if perhaps he hadn't acted with "too much courage." However, "at the end of the day, most of it worked."

Indeed it did. Joachim Faber's talent for recognizing opportunities—large opportunities—and then breaking them down and accomplishing them through succinct, dis-ciplined steps is one of the major keystones of his success.

4

EXPECTATIONS
and
REALITY

28 OCTOBER 1997

JUST A DAY'S REST. That was all. It was hard to fathom, but after descending Mount Meru, we had just one day before we would begin to tackle the ultimate goal we had traveled here for: the challenge of making it to the top of the mighty Kilimanjaro.

Calling it a day of rest was certainly a misnomer. It was more like a day of apprehension. After watching Michael, my experienced guide, nearly perish from altitude sickness the day before on Meru's peak, I naturally wondered how we novice climbers would fare.

The outlook was anything but bright when we set out early the next day in the preternaturally wet rainforest at Kilimanjaro's base. It would have been a beautiful scene under any other circumstances. At present, though, the buckets of rain that were drenching us were greatly diminishing the enjoyment. Our boots became containers of water.

My hair hung over my eyes in dripping wet rat tails. I slipped and slithered over a trail so muddy that I had to walk at half my usual stride. In what was becoming a recurring train of thought, I began castigating myself for lack of preparation. Should I have done more research on the weather conditions? Should I have put less trust in the company organizing the trip? Now it was too late, and we were suffering the consequences. Some members of our group were prepared, with headlights and waterproof Ziplock bags for their clothing. Hans and I had not even considered so much as rain liners for our rucksacks.

When we reached camp that first night on Kilimanjaro, I watched helplessly as the porters dropped our drenched belongings onto a path that resembled a running stream. Everything was soaked through. My expectations of what our first night on this mountain would be like were in a similarly dreary state.

It was too late to beat ourselves up over past actions. We couldn't expect our English expedition leader (I will call him Alistair to protect the guilty) to bail out a couple of idiots who were not adequately prepared for such inclement conditions. (In just one day, I had demoted my self-image from senior vice president to idiot.) In any case, I was also starting to question this particular expedition leader's attitude. He certainly had an imposing set of mountaineering credentials, with several conquered impressive peaks to his credit. This, however, would be his first trip up Kilimanjaro. Knowing that, I watched him closely, and I began to notice small things that alarmed me. He seemed more concerned about his personal agenda than about the group's. It was fine that he had set for himself the goal of conquering the peak no matter what (adding another notch to his own personal mountain of credits), but what about us?

The guide pitched his own tent with enviable ease, even in the rain and terrible conditions. And then he slipped into it. A real leader, I knew from business and pure life experience, would have made sure that his team and the rest of the group were safe and sound under their canvases before he escaped into his own. This confirmed my feeling about him: here was a guy who wanted to make it to the top at all costs, regardless of how the rest of us fared. From the day's start to its finish, the beginning of this journey was not as I'd dreamed it would be.

Over the next few days, the rain did not let up. It worsened, in fact, and the climb only grew more traumatic. Although I'd trained as hard as I could beforehand and prepared on Meru, I was not used to the level of continual physical struggle. Even with the support of the porters and guides, who shouldered the greater part of the gear and luggage, I found carrying my own burden an increasing struggle. My backpack seemed to grow heavier and heavier, and the incessant rain intensified every minor irritation so that I felt a dark animosity growing inside me. I was more than merely frustrated. I was thoroughly miserable.

So far, we had alternately trudged and leapt through torrents of water, waded through sticky mud, crept forward under the burden of heavy packs, and endured limited visibility that hid the most scenic part of the mountain—the trail—from our sight. Magnificent views? Mine was of the backside of the climber in front of me as we stumbled through the clouds and the mist and the rain. If we were not inching up or sliding back on mud, we were struggling over boulder-filled plains or laboring across the crumbling face of rock. Marathon-trained runners wouldn't have had an easier time with this constant slipping and sliding. Extreme focus and agility were required, and I knew it was just a matter of time before someone got injured.

To my horror, that someone turned out to be Hans. On the second day, he slipped and tumbled onto some rocky debris. While trying to break his fall, he jammed his ring finger straight into the ground. His beautiful, masculine hands, which I adore, now looked grotesque, with the dislocated ring finger on the left hand pointing backward.

I watched the color drain from Hans's face. It was not a life-threatening injury, of course (and Hans would never let such an injury get in his way anyway), but the doctor accompanying us was infuriating. He acted with a marked lack of sympathy and did just the bare minimum to treat the injury. Again, I began questioning the leadership on this journey. For the first time, I truly doubted whether it was even safe to continue in these conditions. Alistair, the expedition "non-leader," as Hans called him, had already escaped to his tent. He did not seem to entertain any such worries, and I tried to suppress my doubts for the moment at least.

Matters came to a head at the end of the third grueling day up the mountain. At 4,200 meters, we had reached the Barranco Wall. Technically, the mountain guides told us, this would be the most difficult part of the climb. It was a wall, quite literally, a flat face of sheer granite. Would Hans be able to climb it? Could his injured hand support his weight? Alistair seemed neither to question the outcome nor to care very much about it.

I sought out one of the Tanzanian guides, a man named Tobias, for advice. He had impressed me with his enduring calm throughout the past three days. What did he think, I asked, about the conditions for tomorrow's climb?

"They are terrible," he said frankly, with no hesitation. "Very, very dangerous."

"So why are we climbing, then?" I asked.

He shook his head and confirmed my suspicions. "I suggested to Alistair that we should turn back already, but this Englishman is stubborn. He won't listen to me." Tobias shrugged. "The company put him in charge, and the company pays us to take orders from him. What can I do?"

I took a long, hard look at the Barranco Wall, barely visible in the rain and the gathering dusk. Tomorrow, the company expected Hans and me to scale that wall—even though a highly experienced local guide apparently thought it too risky to continue. The man who was leading us, the man who was responsible for our safety on the mountain, had ignored the expert advice of a guide who, unlike himself, had actually made this climb before in all varieties of weather.

My thoughts echoed Tobias's earlier refrain: "What can I do?" Only instead of saying it in despair, I was searching for an answer. I had been a leader throughout my childhood and up through the corporate ranks. Instinctively, I knew what to do. But could I do it?

LEADERSHIP LESSON NO. 4:
THE ATTRACTION OF PREPARATION

When I was a schoolgirl in my native Transylvania, I worked very hard. I was a straight A student, but not because I was a born genius. Rather, I spent many hours studying and preparing for the next day's lessons. I went to class in the morning, and in the afternoon I generally helped my mother in the vineyards. The evening was allocated to schoolwork. If I could not finish my assignments before bedtime, I asked my mother to wake me up at 5 a.m. to finish them then. The possibility of going to class unprepared did not even occur to me. I did whatever it took to accomplish what needed to be done.

If you want to be at the top of your game in anything, you must prepare and practice, put in the hours. There is simply no substitute for hard work. Only in the dictionary do you find *achievement* and *success* before *work*. Overnight successes only seem that way. Behind every shining success lies a great deal of planning and preparation. Confucius said it best: "Success depends upon previous preparation, and without such preparation, there is sure to be failure." Dr. Robert Schuller, one of America's great possibility thinkers, adds a modern twist that drives home that point: "Spectacular achievement is always preceded by unspectacular preparation."

Margaret Thatcher, now affectionately called "Lady T" by those close to her, is one leader who made a science of preparation. Recently I had the privilege of cohosting a small lunch at which Lady Thatcher was the guest of honor. As is customary, in preparation for the event we had submitted the biographies of the guests to her office. During lunch, we made sure that everyone had the opportunity to sit next to her, and when my turn came, I was quite eager to ask her what factors contributed to her success.

Mrs. Thatcher gave me three answers. "My parents taught me the importance of hard work," she said, pausing for a reflective moment afterward. "Second, integrity. People may not like what you stand for, but they have a right to know what you stand for." Finally, she put her hand on my arm and looked me straight in the eyes. "Like you, I am a tax lawyer by training," she said. "And I always know my facts."

I was speechless. Here was Margaret Thatcher, in her early eighties, and she knew my background. She had worked hard. She was prepared.

RUTHLESSLY PREPARE

It is not enough just to prepare for the obvious. Preparation means assessing the entire situation that presents itself and, most important, the human beings that are around you. It means planning for contingencies and looking at the details in the most objective way possible, while never losing sight of the big picture.

Of course, there is a limit to what you can prepare for. You can prepare for the best, and you can prepare for the worst. You cannot prepare for the unforeseen, but you can plan for the outside chance that the unforeseen might happen—that way, you have time during an event to deal with the unknown.

However, you cannot prepare for everything. Make sure you surround yourself with people who complement your weaknesses, and then have the confidence to delegate to others in areas where you are weakest. (We will examine this aspect further in later chapters on team dynamics.)

Sometimes, even though you work hard, you may not get the payoff that you expected or deserve. You need to be aware of your strengths and weaknesses, and then work hard in areas where you are strong. In addition, you may identify knowledge gaps where you need to improve. In my case, I had solid legal training, but while I was working at Citibank in London, I felt that I needed more education on the business side. While working full time, I enrolled in the executive corporate finance program at London Business School, a course that stood me in very good stead when I made the transition from law into front-line investment banking.

As William Osler once said, "The best preparation for tomorrow is to do today's work superbly well." Our Kilimanjaro climb illustrated this beautifully. Anyone can (and must) prepare for important events. A wedding, a trip, or a climb up a mountain—these occasions all merit a lot of planning. Try your best to cover every contingency. What if it rains? What if someone is injured or dies? What will we eat? Where will we go to the bathroom? These things are important.

Lawyers typically are great with what-if scenarios. In law school, we are taught to analyze a problem from all sides. That's because we (or, actually, our client) could be on either side of an issue. Contingency planning is a key line of thought for lawyers. It should also be a key line of strategy for executives who are maneuvering their way to the top. How should you deal with a toxic boss? What if the economy tanks? What if the equipment doesn't work at your presentation tomorrow? In other words, never underestimate the importance of a backup plan.

However, it's also important to be flexible. Even though I strongly recommend planning for all possible scenarios, it is also important that you remain flexible. If you have planned for a scenario, and your plan just isn't working the way you imagined it, then you have to be open to changing course. It doesn't benefit anyone to remain locked into a course of action that will lead to certain failure.

With the idea of changing course in mind, it's important to learn how to improvise. It is impossible to plan for every scenario down to the minute detail. Sometimes life will throw you a curveball, and you'll just have to improvise. Do your best—or rather, hope for the best, but plan for the worst. Then you can move forward with confidence. As Arthur Ashe said of self-confidence: it is "one important key to success. And an important key to self-confidence is preparation."

▸ *In conversation with* ◂
BARONESS SCOTLAND OF ASTHAL

No one exemplifies preparation better than Patricia Scotland, also known as Baroness Scotland of Asthal. Her climb to the top from humble beginnings on a Caribbean island has been a significant achievement, affecting the lives of millions. She was the first black attorney general in the United Kingdom and the only woman to serve in this position since it was created in 1315.

I initially met Patricia through our mutual interest in the empowerment of young people, particularly through the Prince's Trust. My assessment of her as a person who is always prepared and puts others first was proved accurate nine days after she was appointed attorney general. Months before her appointment, she had agreed to speak on a panel on faith and politics that I was chairing in London at the House of Commons. On that day, I was wondering whether she could come, since she had been at her post for such a short time. I should not have worried. Even though she had slept only 27.5 (the half was important) hours in 9 days, she came prepared and ready to give of herself!

The tenth of 12 children, Patricia's aspirations to help people, she told me, began early. She decided as a child that the best way for her to do so was to become a lawyer. "I really thought that in being a lawyer, there was an opportunity to help other people."

Patricia has done exactly that. As a member of the House of Lords and at one point a parliamentary secretary in the United Kingdom, this lawyer was responsible for intense work involving the reduction of domestic violence. She introduced what is known now as the Crime and Victims Act, the act that made possible the recognition of familial homicide in the United Kingdom. Barristers have famously used this act to prosecute killers who might have escaped prosecution without it. By 2009, domestic violence in the United

Kingdom had fallen by 64 percent, and the domestic homicide rate in the United Kingdom was at its lowest in 10 years.

"I thought I would really like to be a lawyer, but there weren't many women lawyers at the time, and there were even fewer black women who were lawyers," she said. On her journey to achieve this goal, many discouraged her. Patricia was in her mid-teens when her family moved to London. "At school and elsewhere, they were quite discouraging about that, but I received my law degree at 20, qualified as a barrister at 21, and started practicing." By 1999, a relatively short time later, Baroness Scotland was the Parliamentary Under Secretary of State, where she oversaw the United Kingdom's relationship with all of North America and the Caribbean, in addition to being in charge of parliamentary business at the House of Lords. As a young Member of Parliament, she introduced the Pro Bono Lawyers Panel, a group of U.K. lawyers who worked for free to help U.K. citizens who were imprisoned in foreign countries.

In 2003, then prime minister Tony Blair put her up for consideration as the leader of the House of Lords. And the next year, she was a candidate to become commissioner of the European Union.

This is a woman who knows how to manage her goals and her career choices carefully with the key tool of preparation—make that *assessment* and preparation. She told me that, to prepare for a career that many around her thought was unreachable, she was forced to adopt a mindset of preparation and analysis.

It is important "to be very clear about what you think success looks like in terms of outcome, and then prepare to do the work necessary, to do the analysis necessary, to enable you to get what you really want. It takes a lot of commitment." Analysis and commitment are two of the key traits that define Patricia. This is how she got where she is today.

In the earliest days of her career, Patricia decided to treat every case "as if it were the only case I would ever do." Having such a mindset meant intense preparation around the clock. She knew that only an exemplary track record of excellence as an attorney would be proper training for her true goal: getting to a place in her career where she would be capable of helping the most people. "For me, what was really important was what I wanted to achieve—it wasn't about me. I think if I had thought I wanted to become the youngest Silk [Queen's Counsel, that is, a lawyer appointed by the Crown] or I wanted to go to the House of Lords, I would not have gotten there. What I did was think about outcomes."

Treating every case as if it were the only case she would ever work on was a mindset that allowed her to prepare for each case in the best way possible, too, she said. "So it would not be only preparing the case properly, but it was also really getting to understand the case from my client's point of view. I would say to them: 'I need to be looking through your eyes, hearing with your ears, and speaking with your mouth to understand what happened to you. That way, when I come to represent you, I am fully briefed, and I really understand.'" This intense preparation for each case helped to ensure the outcome she desired.

For Patricia, concentrating on outcomes encompassed her father's advice to leave the world a better place than she found it and to never be afraid to be an agent of change. Concentrating on outcomes meant following her dreams. Obstacles stood in the way of Patricia, a black female barrister in a largely white male profession. As previously stated, she is the only female U.K. attorney general in that post since England created it in the 1300s!

More than anything, though—more than the focus, the tireless work, the ignoring of those who decried her goal— Patricia says that intense preparation was key to her success. She believes, as I do, that it is a key ingredient for all executives seeking serious positions of leadership.

"You have to say to yourself, Where am I now? Where do I want to go? And in order to get there, you've really got to do the analysis—your needs-based assessment of what you need to have for success. All of that is preparation. Then you have to factor in things that are unexpected. And if you really understand the whole of the waterfront of your subject, then you are able to deal with the unexpected more easily. Because you have choices."

Patricia gave an excellent example of this from her earliest days of practicing law. She told me, "From the age of 20, I had been involved in family law. And it seemed to me that you could change domestic violence and change the incidences of domestic violence, something many people said was impossible." Lots of people told her that she couldn't do it, that domestic violence is like the poor—it would always be there. "Because of the work I had done, I knew that that wasn't true. I also knew that if you prepared properly and if you were able to identify the phenomenon early and cut it off, then you could reduce the level of domestic

violence. So when I was made the chair of the interministe-
rial group (a committee of ministers of all government departments chartered to coordinate and implement policy),
the first thing I did was to ask for an economic assessment
of the economic cost of domestic violence." And Patricia
was instrumental in introducing bills and making changes
that did in fact reduce domestic violence in a major way. Her
method? Assessment of the facts, and then ruthless preparation.

Finally, it is important to be able to leverage those around
you in your journey to success. Patricia exhorts executives
to ask themselves important questions, such as "What do I
need if I am to enable this team to help me do what I want
to do? What are the obstacles in the team members' way that
make it more difficult for them to help me? What is our common ground?" She grew up with a Catholic father and a
Methodist mother, and her parents had taught her to focus
on what unites people, not what divides them. "What are suggestions I can make and actions I can take to help them to
take care of some of these obstacles? Or can I help them see
that in fact the obstacles are not what they think?" she said.
"That is all preparation and analysis."

5

TURNING
BACK

THE CONFIRMATION from our Tanzanian guide, Tobias, had proved that I was right—the conditions were in fact too dangerous to continue. Now I was left in an agony of indecision. I still wanted to achieve my dream and reach the summit, yet Hans was already hurt, and any one of us could be next. I didn't want any injuries—or worse—to be the result of my overarching ambition. Didn't I have a responsibility to the other climbers to share what I'd learned about the danger we faced?

Also, I was angry. Alistair seemed to be focusing on his own ambition to reach the summit so that he could add another line to his mountaineering résumé. Maybe an experienced climber like him had seen conditions such as these or worse, but the rest of us were amateurs—essentially enthusiastic tourists. He was putting us all in serious danger. How could he be so self-centered and careless? Certainly, we'd all signed up for this adventure, but we weren't out to conquer the summit at any cost.

At least it wasn't raining anymore. However, our bags sat sadly in pools of water, and Hans and I had not fared much better. Despite his injured finger, he'd erected a tent and inflated the mattresses. But we awoke wet, cold, and shivering. Amazingly, there were some dry clothes in those soaked bags, and I extricated them with a feeling of deep gratitude and relief. There were just two sets of dry clothing: one set for Hans and one for me.

Once we were clothed and ready for the day, it was important that Hans know everything about the conditions of our climb. I told him everything, and also about my indecision regarding leaving too early. To my relief, Hans immediately agreed that we should leave, and we decided to tell the others. "We'd better get it over with and tell the rest of the group right away," he added. "Some of them will be glad to have someone else take the initiative and say we've reached our limit. They'll want to come back down with us."

What a comforting thought. And in fact, it was true. I joined the rest of the climbers and told them about my worries regarding conditions and that we planned to go back down. I saw relief in the faces of several climbing with us, and they said that they, too, would be joining us. There were others, though, who insisted on staying on course. They apparently felt that it would be wimpy to admit defeat. At the time, I thought, well, maybe they're right, and we can help one another up to the peak, even under these conditions. But maybe they weren't.

I am not a timid person. Back at the office, my colleagues and employees would have laughed at the idea of my backing down. Being timid here—caving in and keeping up the climb to the top—would mean being swayed against my better judgment. It could risk our very lives!

"This is why people die on mountains," Hans muttered to me as we began readying ourselves for the descent. He was right. Continuing on the path we'd started on would have led to an unsatisfactory result. I had seen it time and time again in my personal life, at work, and now here—people getting so obsessed with reaching the top that they cut corners and took irresponsible risks. In this case, such risks could be fatal. And in fact, people do die on Kilimanjaro every year.

Despite my firm decision and my comfort with it, it was still wrenching for us to pack our rucksacks that morning while watching the rest of the group prepare to climb the Barranco Wall. As we started back, accompanied only by a junior Tanzanian guide who probably had a Swahili name, but who called himself John, I felt lonely and utterly regretful. The rest of the group had decided to go on, several of them expressing the pressure they felt to continue, but for me it was the end of a dream. However, I kept telling myself that I would be back.

We descended at an alarming rate on an ultra-steep trail designed for medical evacuations or other emergencies. John told us that we'd be down in six hours—shocking, considering that it had taken us three days to get up this high in the first place. We had water supplies with us for those six hours. I hoped he was right. We slipped and slid through boggy mud at a breakneck speed, hanging on to handholds where we could, for fear of ending up smashed and dead at the bottom of a sheer drop. Despite the speed of our descent, it became apparent by lunchtime that six hours was an underestimation. By 7 p.m., after 10 hours, John's reassuring smiles were beginning to fade; it was pitch-black, the slope was still slippery, and we had run out of water.

We were exhausted, hungry, and thirsty, and I am not ashamed to say that I was also afraid. To make matters worse, John's flashlight started to fail and finally died. Now we had to share the remaining flashlights. We kept going, walking and sliding, with the occasional bone-chilling roar of a lion in the distance. There was no thinking of stopping. The only way to survive this experience was to keep going—to keep stumbling and slogging farther down.

I had lost all track of time when I heard what sounded like a woman's voice, calling for her children. Suddenly we saw it—a little gatekeeper's hut at one of the entrance gates to the mountain. Every muscle in my body collapsed with relief. This wasn't the end of the trail, but thankfully we were safe for the time being. Moments later, from out of nowhere, we were surrounded by people staring at us like animals in a zoo. But then, what other reaction could they have had? We were in a terrible state—cold and wet, and also emotionally and physically exhausted. I tried desperately to think of the Swahili word for water.

Fortunately, I'd seen Coca-Cola signs plastered all over Tanzania, so I tried that. "Coca-Cola, please," I said. The woman, who had brought us stools, looked at us, smiled in resignation, strapped her baby to her back, and began walking away from us. I was too out of it to realize what was happening, but Hans realized it immediately. She was prepared to hike several kilometers just to get us some soda! He jumped up and showed her our empty water bottles, and I could see understanding dawn on her face. She led us to the well, and we drank.

The kindness of that Tanzanian woman remains with me to this day. She invited us to stay, but with an unusual urgency in his voice, Hans spoke up: "Hotel! Please!" I didn't blame him. By midnight, the villagers found an accountant from the nearby town of Arusha who was visiting the village, and for $100 that kind man drove us to the nearest hotel.

Later, in the hot water of the shower, with tremendous relief, but also with traces of disappointment plaguing me, I began to understand. In life and in business, there are times when failure is acceptable. In fact, it can even be a learning point and a stepping-stone.

There is a famous story regarding the mountaineer Sir Edmund Hillary. The first time he failed to conquer Everest, he shook his fist at the mountain and shouted: "You're not getting any bigger, but I'm still growing."

Two days later, as we drove away from the hotel and toward the airport, I looked once more at Kilimanjaro, glittering in the distance. I was still in love with the sight of it, and with my dream of reaching the peak. I was not going to give up. Nor was I going to shake my fist at it, Hillary style. I was going to try again, no question. Hans agreed with me in full. We were resolute. The driving rain, the mud, the danger, the fear, the ultimate decision to fail on our own terms—this was all just a prelude to the longer journey, I knew.

I had just turned 40. It would be 10 more years before I returned.

LEADERSHIP LESSON No. 5: FAILURE

True success is often a matter of braving failures and bouncing back. The key is not throwing in the towel when you hit a wall (or when a wall hits you like an avalanche). The first leadership lesson, on resilience, stresses the importance of bouncing back. You must have the strength, will, and desire to bounce back when things don't go as planned. The other half of the equation is simply accepting that failure is a part of any journey.

Admitting the failure is the first step. Denying it and continuing along a doomed path can be fatal to your career. It is so easy to stubbornly refuse to admit that what you're doing isn't working. This is something that Winston Churchill directly addressed when he said, "I'd rather be right than consistent." Most seasoned leaders will probably tell you that admitting failure and changing course to another, more fruitful method is a key element in their success.

Dwelling on your failures and looking back, rather than forward, is another common mistake that executives make. One morning over breakfast, I was beating myself up over some stupid decision that I had made at work. My husband listened quietly, offering neither advice nor condemnation. When I looked at my BlackBerry on my way to the office, though, he had texted me the following: "Do you know why the windshield on a car is so large and the rearview mirror is so small? Because the FUTURE is a lot more important than the past." The lesson is clear: when you fail, make sure that you don't dwell on it. Fail fast, learn everything you can, and move on. This requires courage and a certain amount of wisdom, to be sure. It is tempting to suffer and sulk in the mire of your failure. Yet it is self-defeating to do so.

FAIL FAST AND FAIL FORWARD

There will always be people around you—jealous colleagues, conniving up-and-comers, threatened leaders on the way down—who are ready to use your failure as a dagger. It is anything but. Each failure breeds more learning and gives you a fresh frame of reference for a new beginning. Not only does failure lead to personal growth, but it leads to success. The more you fail, the more you are trying. Don't give up. Give failure its proper role in your mind: a place to dwell briefly, learn and reflect, and move on from quickly.

After a successful career in investment banking, I decided to set up a private equity firm focused on sustainable investments in frontier markets. While my vision for the firm was compelling and our value proposition was timely, I did not understand the industry well enough to avoid several major mistakes. At one point, everything I had worked for seemed like sand running through my fingers. In trying to salvage what was worthwhile, I mentioned to one of my investors that we still had a lot to work with. His damning assessment hit me right in the solar plexus: "We have the square root of nothing," he said and pulled his financial backing. Failure! Utter failure! The pain is indescribable. And yet, it seems, failure is the best teacher.

Frame your failure not as a failure or an endpoint but as a necessary pause in your path to arriving at your eventual goal. Ignore those naysayers around you who will, out of jealousy or through their own fear and incompetence, frame your failure as the end of the road. It is the beginning. In failure, there is learning. There is also great opportunity for growth.

Thomas Edison gave what I think is probably the most insightful quote about failure. On his long road toward inventing some of the most important technologies we use today, he said, "I have not failed. I've just found 10,000 ways that won't work." It was Edison, after all, who first put the term *failing forward* into popular parlance. Discussing the errors of U.S. President Woodrow Wilson, Edison concluded, "They say President Wilson has blundered. Perhaps he has, but I notice he usually blunders forward."

The playwright Samuel Beckett echoed that sentiment when he advised, "Try again. Fail again. Fail better." If fear of failure is hampering your ability to achieve your potential, please stop now! Ask yourself why. If you cannot figure it out, go and talk to a counselor or a trusted advisor.

Is this easier said than done? Of course. Success isn't easy—that's why so few people reach great heights. The vast majority of people are easily discouraged by the inevitable failures that a road to success includes. However, if they chose instead to view failure as an opportunity to begin again with a fresh perspective, it would be amazing how many more people would succeed.

Organizational researchers Adrian Wilkinson and Kamel Mellahi, writing on behalf of England's Warwick University and Australia's Centre for Work, Organisation and Wellbeing at Griffith University, say that psychological literature is full of studies about how and why some executives are able to learn and move forward from failure, while others aren't. It is a complex phenomenon, they conclude, but one that underlies the strategic success of individuals, teams, groups, and companies. They say that the culture of an organization largely determines whether the individuals within it are able to fail fast and fail forward. That doesn't mean that you should let your organization determine your ability and outlook regarding setbacks. In the end, it is up to you to take the right attitude, admit failure, accept it, learn what you can from it, and move forward.

▶ *In conversation with* ◀
MARSHA SERLIN

There are few executives I know who are more determined and more driven than Marsha Serlin. From facing the foreclosure of her home and struggling to feed her children, she now presides over one of the largest industrial recycling companies in the United States, as the CEO of United Scrap Metal, a $215 million company that processes more than 140,000 tons of steel every year.

Rising from the ashes of economic ruin, Marsha founded a recycling company before recycling was a buzzword. She looked at the scraps of metal lying around her neighborhood and pondered how she could build a business around them—and then she did. She started her company after finding a neighbor who knew the business and "asking him to tell me everything he knew about it in 24 hours."

United Scrap Metal, Inc., was established in 1978 as an independent, privately held scrap metal recycler. Marsha developed the business from an initial $200 investment to one of metro Chicago's largest and fastest-growing full-service recyclers. She worked 16 hours a day, looking everywhere for scrap metal. By 1981, her company had an actual headquarters in Chicago, and today, she employs hundreds of employees with, she says, an extremely low turnover rate.

United has become recognized as one of the most energetic and innovative companies in the scrap metal industry. Its reputation for professionalism and exemplary service has led to long-term relationships with many of the Midwest's top industrial companies.

When I spoke to Marsha about her experiences, she was on her boat in the Bahamas, knowing full well that her company was in very good hands after she had appointed her son as president.

"At United," Marsha explained, "we are providing clients with the right service, at the right price, and in the easiest way possible." Her business approach has garnered her wide industry recognition. She is the recipient of numerous awards, including her selection as a finalist for Ernst & Young's 1997 Entrepreneur of the Year Award and as the recipient of the 1997 Grant Thornton Executive Woman of the Year Award.

Failing fast and failing forward is a philosophy that continues to be one of the major keys to Marsha's success.

"Taking risks is part of living, and you can't move unless you take some risk," Marsha told me. Admitting that fear of failure is often an ingredient of risk taking, she states that the thing is to move past it. "I move past fear as fast as I can because I can't afford in my life to live with and to think about regrets. I want to do it all, to get there, and I just want to move forward."

Rebounding from failures, large and small, is essential to success. "So many times, great ideas come from simple things that you notice. And the next time, I'll say, 'Let's try that another way. What could we do differently from what we're doing now that could create more of a success?'"

It's up to leaders, she added, to create an environment in which failure is safe, and learning and recovering and rebounding from failure are possible. "If you're going to knock somebody down every time he comes up with an idea, then he's going to stop giving you ideas. But if he feels safe, then he can contribute. That's when he wins, and that's when you win."

Inspired by Winston Churchill, Marsha reminds herself that "Courage is going from failure to failure without losing enthusiasm." This advice is timeless.

"The past is not a blueprint for the future; it's not the way it's supposed to be. . . . You make your own life," she mused. "I look back on my life and think that, whenever I thought I was golden, life slapped me in my face. Life has a way of slapping you every once in a while." She had built the business to being a formidable service provider when she decided to diversify. It proved to be a very costly endeavor, and she lost millions of dollars. "But I was resilient; that's when I moved forward and said, 'Okay, so I made this big mistake, but it's not going to stop my business.'"

The most important part of failure, then, is to recognize your mistakes and move past them quickly. Failure is the best way to learn.

"It's not where you start, it's where you finish," she stated firmly. "And surely I'm not done, not even now."

6

The
LONG PAUSE
BETWEEN

AFTER ABORTING MY first attempt to summit Mount Kilimanjaro, I went back to London, and I was busier than ever. I'd dedicated a good part of my lifetime to my career, and there was always plenty to be done, so it wasn't long before I was thousands of miles away from Kilimanjaro—not just physically, but mentally, too.

My career had been on the fast track right from the beginning. Even though my immigrant parents could barely understand how important getting into the right school was, everything fell into place. I graduated from law school in Michigan at the height of the recession in the early 1980s, and I was the first in my class to land a job, starting work as a consultant just three days after my last exam. Several years later, I enrolled at New York University's School of Law, getting my LLM in International Taxation.

Perhaps my constant striving to get to the top was a form of overcompensation. After a youth of poverty and oppression in Communist Romania, where I had even been kicked out of school for my parents' religious beliefs, I needed a sense of identity. My ambitions and constant work must have been all about proving myself. To me, capitalism, despite its faults, was a far more equitable system. And America, with its enlightened Constitution and its freedom of religion and speech, was a beacon of hope and light. It allowed me to make a difference. In the gray world of social engineering and seven-year plans—the world of Communism—of course my success would not have been possible.

In my new home in America, success seemed not only possible but practically inevitable. During the 1980s, my rise in the corporate world was quick and highly rewarding. I worked around the clock, fueled by heady deals, and I climbed rapidly up the ladder in the corporate world. By 1990, I had earned the opportunity to move into a coveted expatriate posting at Citibank in London. At a point when Citibank's future looked uncertain, I led the effort in Europe to drastically reduce the bank's tax liabilities. It was during my almost 10 fabulous years in London that I spent my fortieth birthday *not* reaching the summit of Mount Kilimanjaro. I was not used to failure.

Maybe that's why I couldn't rid myself of an obsession with that mountain. Sometimes, as I ran through the rain of London at twilight, chasing a taxi or racing to an appointment, it would come back to me: the struggle through the jungle downpours; rain bouncing off rainforest leaves; mist rising off the sodden ground. On the one hand, the memories were ethereal and hallucinatory, far removed from my everyday business pressures. On the other, something nagged at me. I had survived and made it most of the way up the world's tallest freestanding mountain, turning back only because of the weather. I had proved that I could adapt to most adverse conditions and that I was physically fit. There seemed to be nothing left to prove. Or was there?

Meanwhile, my career kept commanding my attention. I moved from Citibank to JPMorgan and eventually to a position at AIG Financial Products, the investment banking arm of the insurance giant American International Group, where I was a managing director. The millennium was drawing to a close. I had survived the dot-com crash, and the world was carrying on as usual. My early forties gave way to my near fifties uneventfully. Except, in my dreams , I caught glimpses of that Rose Glow that I'd seen while I was on the summit of Mount Meru years before. Finally, I realized that I just could not let go of it.

Or perhaps it was the mountain that wouldn't let go of me. In London, rushing through the rain to get to an appointment, I'd remember the rain of Kilimanjaro, the droplets glittering on jungle leaves. These reminders made me feel as though I still had something left to prove. There was no getting away from it: Kilimanjaro was unfinished business. Without entirely admitting to myself what I was doing, I began training again—going to the gym more than usual and getting fit enough to make another run at tackling the mountain.

Everything seemed to click into place. I was not happy at AIG, even though as managing director I had built a very successful structured finance business with multinational corporations. That business had gone from zero to $50 million in net revenue per year. However, it was post-Enron, and the scandal had left a rotten taste. It seemed to me that AIG was no longer the place for me. I had achieved what I wanted to achieve, and I genuinely did not like the direction in which the firm was going. I started thinking about giving back, about philanthropy. Eventually, such thoughts galvanized me into action: I quit my job—to the amazement and even horror of some of my friends. It was a big move, and it left open a big, gaping question, too: what would I do next?

It was at this point that I became increasingly friendly with Rod Chamberlain. A career coach with a successful banking background, Rod was well acquainted with investment bankers like me. He was used to teasing out of us what we really wanted to do. One day, Rod told me about a charity for disabled people called Enham. He was the new chairman for the program. He thought it was just the sort of organization I would enjoy being involved with, so he invited me to take a look.

Enham is, in fact, extraordinary. Its motto, releasing potential, perfectly describes its mission. Founded in 1918, the organization offers a wide range of services to disabled people, helping them with personal development and employment opportunities. The charity's roots are in post–World War I efforts; it was founded to help disabled servicemen. Enham's center, in North Hampshire, England, offered homes and workshops so that these servicemen could rebuild their lives. Later, a development program within the charity evolved to nurture the confidence and skills that disabled people require if they are to make the transition into fully independent living, or whatever lifestyle and employment match their goals and wishes. This program resonated with me deeply. Enham's vision of a society that treats disabled people as individuals and even helps them to achieve their full potential seemed to me a powerful force for good in the world.

I immediately felt an affinity with the people whom Enham was trying to help. After all, all of humanity is striving for something. It is not the nature of their disability that defines people, but the way they strive to overcome it. That's what makes the difference.

As it happened, when I joined its board of trustees as honorary treasurer, Enham was going through a restructuring process and looking for new ways to increase its reach and effectiveness. I could see that it needed a clever way to raise the charity's profile—something out of the box, something different.

It all came together for me one day at the gym. I was pounding the treadmill, with Hans running beside me. Lost in thought, I contemplated Enham and ways to increase its profile. At the same time, an ache in my legs reminded me that the milestone age of fifty was looming for me. Fifty! It was still a while off, but it made me pause. Fifty years. More than half a lifetime gone. Yes, I'd achieved a great deal with my time so far, certainly more than my parents had ever expected in their wildest fantasies, but there was still something missing. Maybe if I could do something for Enham . . .

"Sweetheart." I looked over at Hans and caught a wary look. He slowed his pace. He knew me too well. He had figured out almost as soon as I did that we were on the brink of one of my madder ideas. He would still hear me out as he always did, though.

"I have a great idea," I said, continuing ahead on the treadmill. "You know what I'd like to do for my fiftieth?"

"Let me guess. You want to go back to Kilimanjaro?" Hans asked, as he raised his dark eyebrows. They looked like a big question mark.

"Yes! That's exactly what I want to do. I have something else in mind, too, though. Something even better than that! I want to take a party of disabled people from Enham with me."

And so the mountain and Enham were wed in my mind. It was among my life's most creative moments, marrying my private dream of conquering Kilimanjaro to Enham's need for a higher profile. Of course, it was utterly crazy. As far as I knew, no one had ever attempted such a thing—leading a party of disabled climbers up to the summit of one of the world's largest mountains. There had been previous attempts to reach the summit of Kilimanjaro that had involved a disabled person who was supported by a group of helpers. But a group of disabled people braving the climb? My mind started humming with ideas. What if I teamed each disabled climber with a nondisabled buddy, who could help him scale the mountain? Wouldn't that be a perfect illustration of Enham's goal of releasing the potential in each person? It also seemed as though this would release my own potential, as well. Here I could make a difference in people's lives.

I envisioned a team effort. And within the team there would be mini-teams, coaxing one another along the way, with the able-bodied person helping the disabled and the disabled, in turn, inspiring the able-bodied. I'd attempted Kilimanjaro on my fortieth birthday and failed. What better way to complete the job for my fiftieth than as part of a group like this with support built into it?

Hans thought I was crazy, but I could see the light in his eyes when he told me I'd first have to talk Rod Chamberlain, Enham's chairman, into getting on board. It didn't take long before Rod bit and I had his backing. He took it to the board for final approval, and our adventure began.

LEADERSHIP LESSON NO. 6: YOUR LEGACY

As you climb the ladder to success, it is all too easy to end up in a sort of navel-gazing myopia. It is too easy to become so obsessed with your daily goals, the obstacles you face, and every possible detail concerning your rise to the top that you forget what you are really here for.

Rising to the top and becoming a great leader is what this book is about, true. However, being a great leader also means rising to the top of your ability to be a human being, which involves caring for the humans you serve as a manager and, more widely, caring for humanity in general. As a leader, you have a tremendous opportunity—one that is not afforded to everyone—to invest in your legacy and give back to your community. You may in fact learn that when you are engaged in giving back to the community in a way that doesn't appear to benefit you directly, you are at your happiest.

Investing in your legacy is a powerful and potent action. When you look back and examine your life, you will want to see that you did more than just grind your way to the top, taking no prisoners along the way. After all, when you're gone, isn't it important that you will have contributed something to the world as a whole?

INVEST IN YOUR LEGACY

Choose to invest in your legacy by focusing your efforts, throughout your career and throughout your life, on a worthwhile cause. This is more than tossing a can of food into a "feed the homeless" bin in your local grocery market. It is more than just writing a check annually. Investing in your legacy means that you invest yourself—your time and your skills—into a charitable organization or cause that would benefit most from your passion.

Investing in your legacy just plain feels good. Find a cause or community that is important to you. For me, this world feels truly sustainable when every human being can sit on a three-legged platform:

1. Free education at least up to the tertiary level.

2. Affordable health care.

3. An opportunity to make a living. (Civilized societies do not owe people a living, but we do need to create

meaningful opportunities for citizens to earn what they need to live on.)

Given my background, I decided to focus my philanthropy on economic empowerment (particularly of women) and education. To that end, I traveled all over Africa and India and saw firsthand the importance of empowering people to become entrepreneurs. I also quickly realized that my initial efforts were not enough, and so I began attracting investors in emerging and frontier markets to create jobs for a new generation of young, well-educated men and women.

Charitable organizations greatly benefit not just from your wallet but also from your time and skills as a businessperson and a leader. Some organizations are set up to make "giving" in this way a part of the corporate culture. If you are in a corporate position where you are able to set such priorities, consider doing so. You might follow the example of Target, a chain of stores where each individual location gives 5 percent of its weekly profit back to the community in some way. The shoe company Tom's Shoes donates a pair of shoes to a child in a Third World country for each sale to a consumer. This type of action is incredibly powerful. However, even without any help from your employer, you can choose to invest in your legacy by focusing your efforts on a single cause.

Psychologists have a more elaborate phrase for giving back: "pro-social and helping behavior." Nationally recognized psychology researchers Mark Schneider and Stefan Stürmer refer to it as "doing well by doing good." They believe that there are psychological and potentially even physical benefits from shifting your focus onto others and giving back to your community.

Giving back truly benefits us all in the long run. Civilization could never have evolved without so many of its most able individuals' innate desire to help along the weaker members. It is part of our societal DNA—and it wouldn't surprise me if, as genomic biologists continue to decipher the human genome, it turns out that "helping behavior" is hard-coded into what it means to be human.

Dr. Martin Luther King, Jr., put a similar sentiment eloquently: "We are prone to judge success by the index of our salaries or the size of our automobiles, rather than by the quality of our service relationship to humanity."

Investing in your legacy is much more than charitable giving, as important as that may be. Making a lasting impact can be a result of your career, depending on the nature of your work. I have to admit, though, that my career as an investment banker left me yearning for more. In the cold light of day, I felt that I and my colleagues were extremely well paid for adding very little value to society. We were not building anything, we were not creating anything of value, and it was hard for me to argue that our sophisticated financial instruments improved the human condition. However, once I started thinking about how I could use my financial, legal, and risk management skills to invest in places and sectors to break the circle of poverty, I knew I was on the right path. For the first time in my life, I had aligned my professional interests with my philanthropic ones. I was excited!

My life seemed to take on new meaning. We still have a long way to go as a firm to make a meaningful impact, but I relish this new challenge and opportunity to invest in future generations.

Arguably, you are reading this book because you love your career or your climb to the top and your image of what you'll look like when you get there. But loving yourself enough to be able to give back to your community will enrich you as an executive, a manager, and a leader. You will set the tone for others. And you will be investing in your legacy. There is no price tag that can accurately convey the value of doing that.

▶ *Reflections on* ◀
"BARON" HENRY WILLIAM STIEGEL

I believe that Winston Churchill nailed it when he said, "We make a living by what we get, but we make a life by what we give." Whenever I lose sight of that simple truth, I look back at my husband's famous ancestor, Henry William Stiegel, an early-eighteenth-century artisan in colonial America.

Soon after arriving in the New World (Pennsylvania, specifically), Stiegel began working in Lancaster County at an iron foundry. Although he achieved a great deal of success with the company, in 1763 he made a decision that changed everything. That was the year he produced his first glassware. Stiegel and a partner began operating their own glassworks two years later, employing more than 130 workers and setting up distributing agencies throughout Pennsylvania and later in Baltimore, New York, and Boston.

Stiegel's fortunes soon boomed along with those of the glassworks. In anticipation of the good times lasting forever, Stiegel began to live the colonial equivalent of a newly minted dot-com billionaire's lifestyle. He had three mansions in all, where, quite literally, cannon fire and a musical band heralded him each time he arrived or left. It was during these heady times that people began referring to Henry as "the Baron," in reference to his German roots, of course.

Along with his fortunes and his social status, Stiegel's influence and profile increased, too. Apparently realizing this, he took the sober step of becoming a community leader and a lay delegate to the Lutheran Ministerium in Pennsylvania.

This latter responsibility prompted him to consider what he could do for his workers in Manheim. In 1772, he sold his fellow local Lutherans a plot of ground on which to build a church—for a nominal five shillings. And he decreed that, "in the month of June yearly forever hereafter the rent of One Red Rose if the same shall be lawfully demanded." Workers promptly built the Zion Lutheran Church on the site that Stiegel donated.

Generous though he was, Stiegel was unceasingly extravagant. When a recession hit, the financial situation of the whole area declined sharply and deeply. Money became increasingly tight in the colonies, and taxes became ever more oppressive. Stiegel mortgaged his two ironworks and real estate to build a second glass factory, and he continued to live beyond his means.

In 1774, Stiegel was put in debtors' prison. When he was freed on Christmas Eve, all his belongings were confiscated. In 1776, the new owner of Elizabeth Furnace, the iron foundry where he had initially made his name, gave him employment. When the American rebels won the battle for independence, the manufacturing of cannonballs was discontinued at the foundry, and Stiegel was again jobless. He died in poverty on January 10, 1785.

Stiegel died bankrupt, with nothing to leave to his descendants, but he left two significant legacies behind for everyone. The first legacy is his innovative glasswork. Examples of his work (now known as Stiegel glass) can be found in museums throughout the United States and in collections around the world. These objects, which combined function, quality, and great beauty, were built with the most innovative technology at the time and are featured prominently in the colonial glass section at the Metropolitan Museum in New York City; in the Edison Institute (Henry Ford Museum) in Dearborn, Michigan; and in numerous other museums.

His second noteworthy legacy was the Zion Lutheran Church in Manheim, Pennsylvania, which still serves the community there. It remains a virtual monument to the sustenance of generosity beyond one's own lifetime.

Twice during his lifetime, Stiegel accepted a red rose as the annual rental payment from the church, but this sentimental gesture was virtually forgotten until 1892, a full 120 years after the deed containing the clause was written. At this time, the Festival of the Red Rose was instituted, and a Stiegel descendant was found to receive payment from the congregation.

Since that year, on a selected Sunday in June, the congregation pays the debt of one red rose to a Stiegel descendant, as required in the old deed of 1772.

When Stiegel set up the contract with this church, he was investing in his legacy. More than 200 years after his death, he is remembered today for the quality of his work and, most fondly, for his generosity. When it comes to your legacy, what will you leave?

7

BUILDING
the
TEAM

MARCH 2007

WHEN THE MOTION that would allow me to release the potential of an entire team of climbers came before Enham's board of trustees, it approved the idea, and this launched me into action. It was time to build a group that not only believed in the vision but were also knowledgeable and reliable enough to accept delegation. I knew firsthand how difficult Kilimanjaro was, even with an experienced guide and local porters. Just planning this trip felt like scaling a mountain in itself.

I'd feared for my life that first time on Kilimanjaro, the result of poor leadership. I'd seen altitude sickness up close on Mount Meru, the result of random, unfortunate circumstances. The victim was a veteran, able-bodied climber, which was surprising at first. In fact, as it turns out, several physically fit climbers die on Kilimanjaro every year. Given all this information, I knew that I could not make a single decision lightly here, especially when it came to building the team.

Our Enham climbers would be putting their lives in our hands no matter what, even if they prepared mentally and physically to their maximum capabilities. It was a moral responsibility, as well as a practical one. There had to be nothing short of excellent strategic planning on my end. I had to prepare for both success and failure, even to the extent of getting a media consultant with expertise in crisis management on board—preemptive planning for the worst-case scenario.

I had to zero in on a project leader—an especially key decision. For this, I approached Steve Ballantyne, an English logistics expert, who not only had experience leading expeditions to the most exotic places on earth, such as Outer Mongolia and Papua New Guinea, but who also had worked with disability charities before. I was taken aback when he challenged the notion that Kilimanjaro should be the mountain that we would tackle. He thought there were plenty of other destinations in the world that would be friendlier to an expedition like ours. "The fact is," he added, "I've never climbed Kilimanjaro. But I've climbed many others where I'm certain we'd have a strong chance of bringing most of the team to the top."

My heart sank. I heard my own voice waver as I tried to explain my romantic vision of standing on what was essentially the top of Africa and my absolute desire to conquer that mountain. As I spoke, I began to doubt my intentions. Was choosing Kilimanjaro purely personal? It had never occurred to me to choose a different mountain. I finally conceded, before Steve left, that I'd be open to exploring other ideas and destinations.

But when Steve returned, he surprised me by agreeing that yes, Kilimanjaro was the right challenge. He had done some research, and he now believed that this was a mountain that the expedition could tackle. I felt total confidence in him at this point. If he'd suggested an alternative mountain, I would have been open to it. He didn't suggest one, though, which seemed like the best possible outcome. We had a first-class project manager on board, and that was the first step toward getting a group to the summit.

Given that one of the objectives was to raise Enham's profile, we needed a top-tier media advisor and film director. We also needed a solid medical team. I was delighted that my good friend Jane Atkinson was willing to handle the PR side. She is a world-class professional who rose to prominence when she worked for Diana, Princess of Wales. Another friend, Joanne Sawicki, also became part of the core team. A vivacious Australian living in London, she had founded her own television channel after years as head of programming for Sky Television, one of Rupert Murdoch's companies.

Steve introduced me to Dr. Chris Parsons, a surgeon with a love of mountain climbing and deep empathy for disabled people. His brother had a disability and was cared for by a charity similar to Enham. Helping out with this expedition was Chris's way to give back, as he put it.

With the core team in place, we focused on selecting candidates for the climb. The ideal number was eight at most, each accompanied by at least one able-bodied buddy to help her. We needed the right climbers, but not just any climbers. We needed the right mix of personalities and abilities that would make the team most likely to get to the top. Rather than being inundated with applications from all over the globe, we stuck with Enham and sent just a single bulk mailing with a flyer to measure interest.

I put Steve in charge of our recruitment weekend. The goal was to select people who would have the best chance of reaching the summit, even if it was going to take some luck for them to do it. The point was to give them a life-changing experience without putting their lives at risk, and to give them confidence in the process. Even the climbers who didn't make it to the top, we hoped, would have an unforgettable growth experience from getting as far as they did.

During that weekend, we met the first of our climbers, Liz Curtis, a woman who'd had a nervous breakdown in 2001 and had not left her house since. She'd received a flyer about the project from Enham and thought: what the hell. Later she told me that she was tired of the constant fear that was interfering with her life, and that the description of the climb in the leaflet persuaded her that now was the time to turn things around. In order to meet us, she stepped out her front door for the first time in more than five years and got on a bus! I will never forget the look on her face when I saw her: petrified, but fiercely determined. I knew immediately that she was right for the expedition. She was desperate to change her life, and despite her agoraphobia, she was willing to travel thousands of miles to do just that.

James Smith was a different type of character altogether. Thin, gawky, and bespectacled, he wore a perennially sunny smile. James was autistic and suffered from severe learning disabilities. A resident of Enham since 1990, he was a perfect example of an Enham success story. He had begun with round-the-clock care and now was living virtually on his own. I wasn't sure how he imagined Kilimanjaro and the adventure we planned, but I could see that it excited him terrifically. His open smile and enthusiasm would carry him up at least part of the way, I hoped.

Alex Adams appeared at first to be James's polar opposite. Alex had Asperger's syndrome and wore a dour and worried expression. Also in contrast to James, whose parents were deceased, Alex had a large family that was willing to finance his trip to Africa. I initially worried that Alex's severe depression and required medication might rule him out as a good choice for the trip. He also was a chain smoker, which could be problematic, but his passion for conservation and nature won me over. I wanted him to enjoy the trail that led up the mountain, from rainforest to ice field.

Val Bradshaw had a question mark dangling over her, in my view. It was a question of physical strength. Once an athletic woman, she'd survived a terrible injury after a horse threw her against a tree. Her injured leg was now several inches shorter than the other. Val was feisty and full of sheer grit, but would that be enough? I took to her immediately, however, and I finally determined that if Val retained her winning attitude during the climb, she would definitely make the summit.

Jamie Magee was another accident victim. Felled by a motorcycle when he was just five, he was paralyzed on his left side. He looked much the way a stroke patient does. His determination was noteworthy, though, and his sense of humor was endearing. Jamie's brother wanted to come along also, which was perfect, since every climber on the team needed to be matched with a nondisabled buddy, and Brian was not disabled.

The last person on our short list was James Bridges. On top of a degenerative spine condition, James's tough life had included teenage depression and 16 years of unemployment and homelessness. The members of the selection panel that I assembled shook their heads and said no, he's not right for this. One member of the panel, Jo, disagreed, though. She pointed out that James walked his dog 10 miles a day, despite nearly constant pain from his condition. "He's even run marathons for charity," Jo pointed out. "That says something about him. He has unbelievable strength of character. I say he goes on the trip. He'll surprise you."

When I first met James, I asked him why he wanted to be on the expedition. "I've never been out of the country," he said plainly, without smiling. "I know I don't look like I'm up to much, but I think I can do it; I really do."

There was a snag, though. We had a stipulation that each member on the expedition had to be able to raise £5,000 to cover costs, either through sponsorship or from family. I knew immediately that James would never find someone to sponsor him.

I looked at Hans. He nodded.

"Okay," I said. "How would you feel if my husband and I sponsored you?"

James smiled widely, and it utterly transformed his face. "You really mean that?" he asked.

"We'll adopt you," I said, and the joy on his face almost brought me to tears.

We had assembled our team of six disabled climbers. I felt that they were of excellent caliber. I only hoped that I could match their determination. The next step was to pair each of them with a nondisabled buddy, and there was no shortage of volunteers for these roles. After the selection process was complete, I told Hans how happy I was with our selection committee and the process. The team we had put together was perfect, it seemed, and on top of that, we had the absolute backing of everyone at Enham.

I could not have been more wrong.

LEADERSHIP LESSON NO. 7: TEAM SELECTION

A team is as good as its leader—or better. I'd turn around that old saw and say that a leader is only as good as his team. Having a solid, loyal, and highly skilled team around you is a must as you climb the ranks to ultimate success.

Studies have long shown that the most successful organizations have a combination of strong leadership and teamwork in motion at every level. That may be true on a macro level, but it is also true for you as a leader or as a manager.

Not everyone has the luxury, time, or circumstances to handpick her team, as I did for my trek up Kilimanjaro. More often than not, either you inherit a team or you must make hard decisions. U.S. President Abraham Lincoln, who will live on eternally for his efforts to hold the Union together and abolish slavery, had in his presidential cabinet a team of his greatest rivals for the presidency. He believed that, rather than choosing a group of yes-men, choosing the best-qualified men, even if they had been his toughest opponents, would lead to excellence. In her book *A Team of Rivals*, author Doris Kearns Goodwin painstakingly shows how Lincoln's team became his greatest tool—and how his rivals, for the most part, turned out to be his greatest supporters and, in some cases, his closest friends.

There are less extreme examples of this phenomenon. The main point I want to drive home here is that the quality of your team—each individual member's potential contributions and definitive strengths—will in the end determine your success. Examples of leaders who are successful despite their teams or who work as individual rogues are few and far between. The team is everything.

SELECT A DIVERSIFIED, WINNING TEAM

The best team on the planet won't excel without an equally great leader. It's also true that a great leader serves her team, and the better the service, the stronger the team. It's a mutual relationship. Select a diversified team with complementary skill sets and a winning attitude. Don't hire in your own image. Then take care of your team as you would your family—listen to its members' concerns and take their criticisms steadily. The team will be inclined to do the same for you.

There are, of course, different kinds of teams. Top-down approaches assume that you, as a leader, essentially drive the team's success, with team members being at your beck and call. Research from several universities worldwide shows that a flat team-based approach is more successful, where the leader seeks to serve the members of the team and help each individual work to the best of his ability. Having team members with the ability and the freedom to self-direct when the going gets rough is, to me, ideal.

When selecting team members, it's important that you take into account more than raw ability or the quality of the résumé you have in front of you. Personality counts, too. Having talented but difficult team members who engage in backbiting and playing political games will set you back as much as having a team of cooperative but incompetent people. When you are choosing a team, aim for individuals who are skilled yet still teachable, individuals who can do the work and also play well with others. In the long run, this will save you countless hours of refereeing political infighting, when everyone should be working together with their eyes on one goal. But most important, look for people with strong values and a positive attitude. Skills can be taught and experience can be gained, but integrity and a strong work ethic are qualities that simply cannot be taught, even by an effective, transformational leader.

As I was building Ariya Capital, I found myself struggling to find the right team. When I shared my concerns with one of my advisory board members, he said: "Herta, this is your vision, your money, your reputation. If you have to change the team every week to get it right, do it!"

That is not to say, however, that you need a group of clones. Steven Covey, the leadership expert and author, points out that "strength lies in differences, not in similarities." Make sure that the sum total of the people on your team amounts to the skill set you need, arriving as it does in different packages.

The importance of diversity was highlighted by Professor Lynda Gratton and her team at London Business School. The researchers observed more than 100 teams and measured their ability to innovate. The results were published in a paper entitled "Innovative Potential: Men and Women in Teams" (The Lehman Brothers Centre for Women in Business, 2007) and led to the conclusion that the most innovative teams are gender-balanced: "Where innovation is crucial, companies should construct teams with equal proportions of men and women. . . . Equal gender representation can help to unlock the innovative potential of teams."

Whatever the team composition, you should be able to trust the team you have. The great industrialist Henry Ford was obviously concerned with this principle when he asked: "Why should I clutter my mind with general information when I have men around me who can supply any knowledge I need?" It is an excellent question. Make sure your team is excellent, make sure you can trust and rely on its members, and don't be afraid to make changes to the team if the team dynamics aren't working. Your success depends upon it.

▶ *In conversation with* ◀
DR. KARL (CHARLY) AND LISA KLEISSNER

Charly Kleissner is a philanthropic entrepreneur who utilizes his high-technology background in his venture philanthropy. A veteran of the technology industry, he has spent more than 20 years as a senior executive in Silicon Valley, working with the likes of Steve Jobs. His wife, Lisa, is an architect who set up the Kleissner Group, an architectural and project management firm providing facility solutions for high-tech and biotech firms.

Charly and Lisa have built a very strong partnership, and both are involved with their foundation. The KL Felicitas Foundation is focused on (1) enabling social entrepreneurs and social enterprises worldwide, and (2) advocating impact investing. Charly and Lisa are both passionate impact investors who are working with a diverse group of entrepreneurs in different parts of the world to help them build their enterprises.

Today, they teach workshops and seminars about social entrepreneurship, entrepreneurial leadership, and social enterprises.

I spoke to them about their management style—in particular, the importance of creating, fostering, and rewarding a winning team.

"It's about delegation and trust—enabling your senior managers to do what they need to do," Charly told me. "Delegating, diversity of opinion, transparency of decision making, and respect for everybody . . . are absolutely necessary."

The pair emphasized a move away from the top-down decision-making style of old in favor of a more distributed paradigm and, in that spirit, the importance of authenticity.

"Authenticity and transparency go hand in hand," said Charly. "If people really feel that you are who you are on a genuine level, not a superficial level, then they are more likely to buy into the team vision. They will support it; they will go with it and with you and accept your leadership. And if you couple that with transparency of decision making even in the hardest situation where people might disagree with you, at the end of the day you still retain respect as a leader and a manager."

The team actually creates together, which is an attitude that a leader must foster, Charly said. "As an executive, you think you control the outcome, and it's very liberating and very empowering once that you figure out that you can actually co-create and be able to receive on a level that you would not have imagined before." Lisa added, "I learned early in my career not to be attached to the outcome, but to be much more attached to the development of the team and the team dynamic. Whenever I had the opportunity to work with a broad team, the solution was always much better than it would've been if I had been the only person directing it. It really is about empowering employees to be able to control the projects and bring in other team members and have this open dialogue."

To Charly, both shared leadership and shared vision are very important. The goal should be to "find a team that shares the vision that you have and your values, then enable that qualified and visionary team." But complete alignment can be narrowing, cautioned Lisa.

"If we are working only with team members who are completely aligned with us, that tends to be flat. What we are looking for arc some key values that arc aligned. But we are also looking for people who don't agree with us, because they are the oncs who can bring a fresh perspective," Lisa continued. "When I get on a board or on a team, the person who has the most opposite opinion to mine is the person I'm going to have lunch with right away. Because I'm going to learn so much from him."

"Charly and I have worked together so successfully because he has a real specific style that he developed in the large corporations. I had small businesses. I've worked with large corporations, but you need a very different style to do that when you're working with 15 different companies and a small team. So I think the combination has really been a plus for the work that we're doing with communities, particularly in rural areas, globally."

These partners are looking for people who "are reflective on the one hand, but not paralyzed by analysis—action-oriented people." Lisa also stressed that good teams are made up of people with a "willingness to be vulnerable, and feel good about it and learn from it."

Selecting people with a healthy sense of self, who are willing to "run their own race," is an important exercise for building any team, the duo advised, and self-respect and mutual respect must underline a strong, capable, and diverse team. These are the foundations of successful team building, according to Lisa and Charly.

8

HOLDING
FAST

SEPTEMBER 2007 TO MAY 2008

As SOON AS MY MISSION started gaining some momentum, all the elements began falling into place. The team was assembled? Check. We had a great group of motivated climbers who were ready to go. A project manager had been recruited? Check. We had the excellent Steve Ballantyne on board. A highly skilled core planning team was in place? Check. Now we needed a professional company with the knowledge and experience to help us get up the mountain. This decision was key.

This company would have to handle the logistics of transporting us and our baggage up the trail, setting up camp, and feeding us. After much research, we identified Alpine Ascents International (AAI) as being among the best expedition companies of its type in the world. Generally, the problem with going with the best is likely to be the cost; AAI cut its estimate back a lot for our charity, but it was still too high. We were tempted to find another group that wouldn't be so pricey, and Steve knew of one that he could vouch for. This alternative company was significantly cheaper—its proposal shaved about a third off AAI's cost. Factoring in the price along with Steve's expert opinion that this was a tough, safe, and all-pro outfit, making this decision was going to be a real dilemma.

From business experience, I am well aware that it is often necessary to take a gamble, a calculated risk that you hope will pay off in the long term. Viewed in this way, the competing bid was quite tempting. However, viewed through the lens of what was most important about the expedition (the fact that it would be a dangerous adventure from every angle), the answer was not obvious. Despite Steve's backing, I could not endorse the less expensive option in the end. We could never, in any circumstances, allow ourselves to expose the group to unnecessary danger. With that in mind, I settled on AAI, a standout company with a proven track record in Tanzania as well as perfect safety credentials. AAI had a solid 20-year record, and it had never lost a climber. We would just have to find a way to channel funds so that we could pay for that level of expertise.

Then there was the question of how to record our experiences on the mountain. A feature-length documentary was the way to go, I decided. The mountain was too large for a photo album or a random video. We needed a proper record of everything that would happen on the trail—the highs and lows that we would experience, the camaraderie, the building excitement giving way to the joy we would experience when we reached the peak.

I wanted audiences to have the film as a record of the mountain's true nature and how starkly the expedition contrasted with most facets of the modern world. Also, as a genre, feature-length documentaries were gaining in popularity. Michael Moore and Nick Broomfield were practically household names. Perhaps sales of the film and sponsorships could help with a funding shortfall.

The documentary, as I envisioned it, would reveal something about the human spirit that is hidden in the modern world of texting and satellites, something essential about the power of nature and the strength required of a group of humans to take on that power. It would show our people, disabled and not, enjoying the struggle, battling, and, ideally, succeeding against the odds. This is, after all, what the human condition is all about at a core level. The courage to be human is something that each person needs to muster for himself, regardless of his perceived challenges and strengths. This expedition and its documentary would show that story—it would reveal these incredible people facing not just the mountain outside but the mountain within.

We moved quickly to find a film director, a real professional, who could do full justice to what we were preparing to do. Now I was confident that I had my core A team in place: an experienced project manager, a prominent media advisor, a very good doctor, a multidimensional TV producer, and a highly acclaimed film director. The last was an experienced producer who had worked for numerous major networks, including the BBC. There seemed to be just a few hurdles left, although they weren't small: getting the fitness of the team members up to snuff, and somehow procuring the kind of equipment we would need if we were to get up the mountain.

I remembered the slopes of Kilimanjaro as I'd experienced them years before. The sun hadn't shined on us then, and it couldn't be counted on to do so now. Conditions could be rough. I was unwavering in my insistence that, unlike our previous experience on the mountain, this expedition would offer true transparency. Everyone would be informed about the issues and challenges before and during the climb. We had to be prepared—both physically and mentally.

We made sure that all the climbers had detailed dossiers containing advice on equipment and on what to expect and how to prepare. The issue of how to equip our climbers with the right kind of clothing and gear was keeping me awake at night. I remembered my wet clothes in the rucksack on my first journey up Kilimanjaro and the anxiety of trying to keep a dry change of clothing ready. I was determined that our climbers wouldn't face the same lack of know-how. We needed sponsors, I decided, who would provide the best possible gear and clothing for climbers.

Our fairy godmother turned out to be the outdoor clothing company Blacks. It agreed to provide a complete kit: boots, raincoats, jackets, trousers, backpacks, and the rest. We would be sufficiently clothed. The other main concern I had was to attract corporate sponsors. Camco International came on board, providing much-needed cash and fielding a climber. Camco, is a global leader in climate change solutions, whose founder, Dr. Jeff Kenna, had reached the summit of the mountain about 30 years before, when its cap was still completely snow- and ice-covered.

Finally, there was the training. Steve Ballantyne directed a series of instruction weekends that contained all manner of mental and physical tests and preparation techniques. But emotional and psychological training was also required. On my failed first trip up Kilimanjaro, I had seen firsthand that physical fitness and mental stability were just the bare-bones requirements for getting up that mountain. I had discovered then that one's body will find reserves of stamina and determination, fueled by adrenaline, that will surface when one needs them most. Emotional preparation was just as vital.

We tackled this important step by explaining to the climbers both the dangers they faced and the ultimate rewards of our adventure. We tried to open their eyes to every conceivable risk and eventuality. Of course, we could not spell out the unexpected and unforeseen, but Steve and his team painstakingly spelled out every demand that they knew the mountain might make of us. Everyone needed to know how serious and how difficult this might be.

Just as important, Steve made sure that there was a motivational aspect to the training. Every climber had to understand not only that there might be hardships but also that turning back might be necessary and did not constitute failure. He underlined the importance of the team as a whole—how we each would be helping the others, climbing together as a team, not just as individuals. He continually emphasized that there was no guarantee we would reach the summit. Weaker members might have to turn back to allow stronger members to continue, or some stronger members might have to turn back to support their weaker buddies on their descent. Whatever benefited the team as a whole would determine how and whether we would reach the top.

We booked the trip for July 2008. As our climbers' fitness levels grew, so did their confidence. Recalling my previous journey to the top of Mount Meru, I felt a practice run was necessary. Steve led our disabled and nondisabled climbers on a successful expedition to the peak of Mount Snowdon— at 1,085 meters the highest mountain in Wales, although just a fraction of Kilimanjaro's 6,000-meter size. Still, it marked a huge milestone. We knew we could do this.

Our novice mountaineers were exhilarated by their success, and even I allowed myself a cautious taste of triumph. There was a long way to go, but this time, if we didn't reach the summit, at least it would not be on account of a lack of planning and preparation.

LEADERSHIP LESSON NO. 8: QUALITY

You have probably heard the old saying that "good" is the enemy of "great." Voltaire, in his letters, is credited with that sentiment, but the thinking behind it is age-old. Being good enough is also enough to stop a would-be great leader in her tracks. The temptation to give in is understandable—if everyone says you're doing well enough at something, why mess with a good thing?

This sort of thinking is poison. Being satisfied with run-of-the-mill or even good quality—whether it involves your employees' performance or your own, or the products you use or the life you live—is anathema to success. Thomas Watson, the longtime CEO of IBM, said it best when he warned:

"Whenever an individual or a business decides that success has been attained, progress stops."

This is a lesson that you should know intuitively. How many times in your experience have you seen "good" destroy "the best," personally or in business? If you compromise on quality, even in tough economic times, you will pay—if not now, then later. The tendency toward mediocrity may be imperceptible at first, but it is often tolerating the little things that causes the slide away from excellence. King Solomon admonished his subjects to "Catch for us the foxes, the little foxes that ruin the vineyards."

DON'T COMPROMISE ON QUALITY

Slipping toward mediocrity—accepting "good" when the best is within reach—is exactly what I mean by compromising on quality. Sometimes the phenomenon is subtle and tough to pin down. Keep an eye out for the little things that compromise quality. Don't allow them. The goal is excellence.

Quality can be found in the most unlikely places. When my husband and I visited Mumbai, I was amazed at the work of the *dabbawalas*. Their efficient genius was a sight to behold. According to the *Economist*, the warrior king who defeated the Mughals and founded the Maratha Empire of western India in the seventeenth century, Shivaji Bhosle, is remembered as both a tactical genius and a benevolent ruler.

The direct descendants of his Malva-caste soldiers are also developing a reputation for organizational excellence. Using an elaborate system of color-coded boxes to convey more than 170,000 meals to their destinations each day, the largely illiterate 5,000-strong *dabbawala* collective has built up an extraordinary reputation for the speed and accuracy of its deliveries. Word of its legendary efficiency and almost flawless logistics is now spreading through the rarefied world of management consulting. Impressed by the *dabbawalas'* Six Sigma certified error rate—reportedly on the order of one mistake per six million deliveries—management gurus and bosses are queuing up to find out how they do it. The system that the *dabbawalas* have developed over the years revolves around strong teamwork and strict time management. At 9 a.m. every morning, homemade meals are picked up in special boxes, which are loaded onto trolleys and pushed to a railway station. They then make their way by train to an unloading station. The boxes are rearranged so that those going to similar destinations, indicated by a system of colored lettering, end up on the same trolley. The meals are then delivered—99.9999 percent of the time to the right address.

It was obvious that nothing or nobody could distract the *dabbawalas* from their work. We were asked to watch them quietly and not get in their way. When His Royal Highness the Prince of Wales wanted to observe them, he was allegedly told that they could not spare more than 30 minutes to greet him. Their duty to deliver the meals was more important to them than meeting royal visitors.

Harvard Business School has produced a case study of the *dabbawalas*, urging its students to learn from the organization, which relies entirely on human endeavor and employs no high technology. For Paul Goodman, a professor of organizational psychology at Carnegie Mellon University who has made a documentary on the subject, this is one of the critical aspects of the *dabbawalas'* appeal to Western management thinkers. "Most of our modern business education is about analytic models, technology, and efficient business practices," he says. Goodman notes that the *dabbawalas*, by contrast, focus more on "human and social ingenuity."

We operate by the maxim, "You get what you pay for," assuming that high quality is by definition more expensive. During my years as managing director of structured finance businesses, I learned that using high-quality advisors enabled us to carry out transactions faster and more economically. For example, the law firms we used were often more expensive on a per hour basis, but the total bill was less than it would have been if we had chosen lawyers who did not have the same level of expertise.

The real danger of compromising on quality—on excellence in the highest sense of the word—is apathy. After working hard on a project or on a life goal, it is too easy to grow tired and apathetic. Make a habit of reviewing the choices you make and checking for apathy and a settling-for-less attitude, and change course quickly if you need to.

David Courpasson from Duke University's Fuqua School of Business has delved deeply into such issues as apathy and indifference in the workplace. He has determined that leaders and employees who feel disempowered can easily fall into apathy—they come to feel that no one cares.

As you focus on making choices with excellence as the underlying factor, remember that those you lead are watching you, too. Empower them to know that excellence and a no-compromise attitude toward quality aren't just watchwords. Show them that you will never compromise on quality in even the smallest of choices, and that attitude will spread throughout those in the organization whose lives you touch directly or indirectly. Invest the time and resources to choose great over good—every time, without fail—and you'll reap giant rewards.

▶ *In conversation with* ◀
MARTHA (MARTY) WIKSTROM

Marty Wikstrom calls herself "a great American story," a kid who grew up on the ski slopes and rose to remarkable heights in the fashion and luxury goods industry. Currently chief executive officer of Compagnie Financière Richemont SA's fashion and accessories businesses, Marty knows something about quality. By any definition, she has had a very successful career in retailing and in the luxury goods industry, having worked with Nordstrom in the United States and Harrods in the United Kingdom, as well as being interim chief executive officer of Kurt Geiger Limited.

I have known Marty for years, and everything about her exudes attention to detail and an enduring sense of quality, as you will see. Although she manages some of the most exclusive luxury brands around, she is a private, understated person with tremendous insights.

Marty joined Nordstrom as a salesperson. "At the time," she said, "Nordstrom was a company with $250 million in revenue, and I joined it in the least likely spot in the world to be successful in the fashion business, and that was Salt Lake City. And 19 years later, I was president of a $6.5 billion publicly held organization," she told me. "It is just a great American story." But Nordstrom's, she said, was a company that promoted from within, shared her values, and was just a natural fit.

"Quality means everything to me. Very early, my dad used to say to me, quality lives on long after the price is forgotten," she told me. "We've been in such a throwaway culture. 'I can buy this. I can buy that.' Why wouldn't you buy a great toaster, and then you wouldn't have to buy 10? I think also that popular culture went through a period of time where nobody wanted their grandmother's things or their mother's things. They wanted to buy new this or new that." This attitude, Marty said, was opposed to focusing on that "underpinning of quality."

"I still remember my father, after the end of a ski day, on Sunday night, putting a lick of polish on our ski boots because it was important. I remember the sense of pride and care that we took in certain things. I never wanted lots of stuff. I wanted things that are good. I liked enduring style. I like classic style and things that stand the test of time. And that's probably a real value that goes all the way back to my childhood."

Investing in quality does not just mean choosing high-quality things. It can also mean choosing high-quality people. Marty is always looking for people who are the right "raw material," people who "get up, dress up, show up," whether they feel like it or not, and people with "empathy." "I can't teach people to get up, I can't teach them to comb their hair, I can't teach them to have an interest and a curiosity, and I certainly can't teach them to have a set of ethics. That comes from home. That comes from within. That's their mountain within, and they have climbed that mountain and come to that plateau before they ever get to my door."

The best companies and the best leaders, Marty said, know that "it's not just about the quarterly earnings. It's about investing in the people who are investing themselves in the company."

Leaders sometimes unwisely cut corners when it comes to high-quality people, goods, and services because of financial pressure. When we spoke about the tyranny of quarterly earnings, Marty had very strong views. "It's the pressure on the CEO to return a certain number, rather than to focus on running a company that has deep integrity in the way it deals with consumers," she said. "We seem to be in this rut. And we are sacrificing quality for short-term gain, with little thought of the next year, the next generation, or the world we're leaving behind. When you're committed to making an impact—to investing for the medium to long term—then you work toward growth and you work toward quality."

To Marty, the value is not just in the luxury brands that she manages but in the decisions that are made in the boardroom to protect those brands. "I actually attribute a huge amount of value to the boardroom." During the recent economic downturn, Richemont posted very healthy results, a testament to the quality of its brands and its management. It ensured that it had a strong balance sheet and that it did not need to cut staff. "A lot of the amazing product that was built in some of our workshops, some of it goes back to the Depression, because what our craftsmen had was time on their hands. . . . And so some of the things that are completely magical at Cartier and completely magical at Van Cleef & Arpels and some of our other brands were developed when people had time." Using the time of her people effectively to produce quality is one of Marty's hallmarks.

In addition, commitment to quality needs to be visible and embedded in the DNA of the company. "I think driving toward excellence, however you manage it, whether it's Six Sigma or not, is really important, and anything you measure gets better."

Marty is a business leader who is committed to quality; she does not take shortcuts, she thinks long-term at a time when most CEOs think about the next quarterly results, and she invests in people. In short, Marty is a leader who has decided to "learn, earn, and return" something of quality.

9

FACING
the
UNFORESEEN

JANUARY 2008

I SHOULD HAVE SEEN it coming, but I didn't. In business, I was used to unforeseen problems popping up. Just six months before we were set to go, I faced the first major, unexpected snag: our film director canceled because of personal difficulties.

This was a huge blow. Finding a committed and talented director was vital to me. The documentary was more than simply memorabilia—it was a promotion for Enham, and financially, its success could potentially support our trek through box office receipts. Also, Black's equipment donation came largely as a result of our promise to feature its gear in the film. Finding a replacement on such short notice was going to be rough. It quickly rose to the top of the list of challenges.

Hans managed to find a little-known but rising film director, Kyle Portbury, and recruited him for the job. After we explained the project, Kyle, an effervescent Australian, became enthusiastic and got on board. He had never shot a documentary, but what he lacked in experience he made up for in guts, creativity, and connections. He helped us get the top British cinema composer, Michael Price, to write music for the film. In addition, he identified the top three extreme cinematographers in the world and persuaded one of them to join the team. It was none other than the award-winning cinematographer Gordon Brown, who has the misfortune of sharing a name with the unpopular U.K. prime minister. (At a fund-raiser in London, I mentioned that Gordon Brown was climbing with us, and someone in the back of the room yelled, "Take him with you and leave him there!") However, our Gordon had flash and really knew his stuff.

We were saved. We might have lost a director, but in his place we ended up with a documentary production team that was far stronger than I would ever have hoped for. Relief followed, but it didn't last.

Even as the film crew was coming together, I was distressed to find out that my support base at Enham was beginning to unravel. Despite Rod Chamberlain's continued enthusiasm, the board was beginning to have doubts about the project and seemed to be losing faith in my ability to pull off this expedition. I felt betrayed. The board had originally approved our trek unanimously. I had never questioned or had reason to question its support as I selected our climbers, worked out issues surrounding the documentary, and planned every aspect of the trip. So what had happened?

Mainly, there were financial concerns. In a worsening economic climate, fund-raising for the charity was slow, and paying people like Steve Ballantyne no longer seemed so critical. There was a growing feeling at Enham that the organization should stop wasting money on an unrealistic, unachievable dream. From business, I knew that the best way to deal with people was in a direct way. Explaining things so that people can understand and watching for cues would be the best way to deal with this.

I spoke to Rod. He was still confident about the project. However, the board members weren't so sure. It seemed as though I'd made a fatal mistake when I discontinued my earlier practice of attending board meetings. Once I stopped going, the whisper campaign began to flourish. Because I was no longer there with regular updates, some board members began to lose faith. Some members thought that I was so absorbed in my own business affairs that I wasn't giving the Kilimanjaro project my full attention. They had initially believed that I could carry off the project because they were sure that I was fully engaged. When they felt that I wasn't as engaged, they grew skeptical.

As I got to the bottom of the board's reasoning, my heart sank. It reminded me of how I felt when Hans and I were tumbling down the mountain after our failed Kilimanjaro attempt years before. At the time, the mountain seemed like a dark nightmare, with danger behind every step. I realized that this was how our project looked to the board members, too. They felt that it was out of control and poorly planned, and that true leadership was missing.

I had to find a way to convince the board members who'd lost faith in me that they were wrong. I had to reinstill that faith and trust in the vision. But how?

In the last several months, I'd worked so hard. Pounding the familiar treadmill, ever training for the rigors of the mountain, I thought hard about it. While I was training and transforming a group of unlikely novice climbers, I'd inadvertently transformed a group of enthusiastic supporters at Enham into doubting, even griping, naysayers. It was not enough, it seemed, to have a vision and keep your eye on the ball. I had neglected to reinforce the vision with the board of trustees at Enham. Naturally, the trustees would ask questions. I knew that we were making great progress with our two national sponsors and our team of climbers. Evidently the trustees did not.

So amidst all the other looming anxieties as the time for the expedition grew near, getting the board back on track was an unforeseen challenge.

LEADERSHIP LESSON No. 9:
THE UNEXPECTED

It sounds like a cliché (and it is), but expecting the unexpected is a must-have attitude for every executive who manages a team, leads a company, or is on his way to the top.

Does anything really happen the way we hope it will? We can plan for contingencies. We can try to avoid failure. But, as Yogi Berra famously (and comically) said: "The hardest thing to predict is the future." Who knows what surprises (positive or negative) you may encounter tomorrow or the day after that? The only certainty is that the future will surprise you. Other people will surprise you. Your industry may surprise you. The very worldview that you hold so dear could change irrevocably if a big enough surprise happens. Ask any of those who witnessed the 9/11 terrorist attack in New York or, conversely, found themselves suddenly and unexpectedly rich when the little start-up they ran ended up being purchased by Google.

The future is all about surprises. Expecting them is half the battle. Being ready for the unexpected is the other half. But how can you be ready for something that you don't or can't see coming?

The first thing to do is to release your attachment to yesterday or even an hour ago—hindsight bias, as it is sometimes called. Nassim Taleb, a mathematical trader and essayist, is a specialist in what he calls "Black Swans," that is, large-impact, hard-to-predict events.

In the introduction to an essay he wrote for *Edge*, Taleb is quoted as saying, "Much of what happens in history comes from 'Black Swan dynamics,' very large, sudden, and totally unpredictable 'outlier' . . . Our track record in predicting those events is dismal; yet by some mechanism called the hindsight bias we think that we understand them. We have a bad habit of finding 'laws' in history (by fitting stories to events and detecting false patterns); we are drivers looking through the rear view mirror while convinced we are looking ahead."

Wild uncertainties, as he calls them, face world markets and individual leaders alike. So how do you deal with them? You've got to be ready for the eventuality that something totally new will pop up at some point, helping (or hindering) your own personal blueprint for what to expect next.

This is difficult to do if you have become too far removed from your organization, from your project, or from the key decision makers who can make or break your deal. In order to leverage your skills and achieve the result you desire, you have to be able to delegate to the people around you. However, as a leader, you need to stay prepared to recast the vision, to remind all stakeholders of the objectives. Delegation does not mean abdication of responsibility. By staying close enough to your team and by creating an atmosphere that is flexible enough, you can deal with the unforeseen. Your team may alert you to developments that you are likely to overlook.

Listen to the quiet whispers, keeping an open mind that shows that you are ready to roll with whatever surprise the next minute may feed you, rather than fall apart. Doing so, like many of the lessons you've read about so far, takes courage, discernment, and self-discipline. It's a mindset that is achievable and that must be achieved if you are to lead effectively without losing your marbles when you are confronted with the inevitable surprises that everyone must face.

It also requires a bit of relaxation. You need to recognize that not everything is set in stone, that your blueprints and plans aren't hard-wired for the future, and that you need to be ready for whatever comes.

When I negotiated my package at AIG Financial Products in the summer of 2000, AIG was a titan with a solid triple-A rating, a good defensive growth stock that asset managers wanted in their equity portfolios. The company was on a financially sound growth trajectory of 15 percent year after year. Hank Greenberg, the company's indefatigable chairman

DELEGATE—BUT BE READY FOR THE UNEXPECTED

Sometimes the unexpected occurs and you miss it, allowing the competition to catch on to a new trend or technology more quickly. Watch for new turns of events. Be on top of them before they're on top of you. But above all, be ready. If there's anything you can say for sure about the unexpected, it is that you will face it during your career. And you must be ready to deal with it, for better or worse, when it occurs.

and CEO, was an icon in the insurance industry and beyond. Who would have thought that eight years later, AIG would need to be bailed out by the federal government?

I will never forget those negotiations in 2000. I had another offer from an investment bank that was prepared to pay me guaranteed bonuses that were more than twice what AIG was willing to offer. Nevertheless, I felt that AIG was the better organization. What really concerned me was the fact that a significant part of my bonuses would be deferred and treated as unsecured, subordinated liabilities of AIG Financial Products, a risk that I was uncomfortable with. When I raised my concerns, my future boss laughed. "This is AIG, Herta. Take it or leave it." It turned out that I took it, but I ended up having to leave part of it. What eventually happened would have seemed highly unlikely when I joined the company. Thankfully, my husband and I had decided from the beginning of our marriage never to live beyond our means. When I lost part of my deferred bonuses as a result of the AIG meltdown, it was a significant financial setback, but we were able to recalibrate.

No matter how painful it may be, the unexpected teaches you new lessons. As the ancient philosopher Heraclitus said, "If you do not expect the unexpected, you will not find it; for it is hard to be sought out, and difficult." This is a remarkable point.

▶ *In conversation with* ◀
SAM CHISHOLM

One of Australia's best-known media executives, Sam Chisholm created empires for the country's preeminent media moguls: Kerry Packer and Rupert Murdoch. Sam is the former CEO of Channel Nine Australia and British Sky Broadcasting (Sky), which he built up to become one of the world's leading satellite broadcasters, with listings on both the American and London Stock Exchanges.

Sam is no stranger to making difficult decisions necessary to turn ailing companies around. When he took over the helm of Sky, a pay-TV satellite network, in 1990 it was losing £2 million a week. He merged Sky with its rival, British Satellite Broadcasting, which was losing £8 million a week but possessed a coveted U.K. broadcasting license. Today, Sky has 10 million paying subscribers, is watched by 25 million viewers—39 percent of the U.K. viewing public—and has a market capitalization of £14.5 billion.

A private man, who understands the media and its power better than most, Sam is reluctant to give interviews.

However, he is no stranger to the art of delegation or to dealing with the wildly unexpected both in his work and personal life. He is alive today as a result of a double lung transplant operation, which has given him a new lease on life. I was delighted to be able to talk with him while he was at his cattle ranch in Australia.

"When I took the job at Sky, I knew it was going to be difficult. Sky was failing, and we needed to expand, so we put it together with BSB." The deal shocked the industry. Only two executives were left standing after Sam was forced to cull the entire BSB staff to curtail the hemorrhaging costs of the combined empire. It earned him the title of "the great sacker," but it was this drastic action, coupled with bold programming decisions, that saved BSkyB.

"We were swimming against the tide—people didn't want to pay to watch TV. We had to find another way around. We had to give people a reason to purchase, to make our product a must have." The answer was Movies and Sports. Sam flew to Hollywood and renegotiated bulk deals directly with the studios, ensuring Sky had first TV rights to all the blockbuster films, at a significant discount. Realizing how important soccer was to the English culture, he then went about securing the rights to the Premier League. But he didn't have the money or clout to be taken seriously, so he did something unpredictable—partnering with the BBC. It was a winning combination, as the BBC had only sufficient airtime to show highlights while Sky had multiple channels that needed to be filled with programming; the resulting partnership ensured Premier League coverage of regional as well as main matches.

This same unbeatable formula of Movies and Sports was perfected by Sam during his 15-year reign at Channel Nine—Australia's number one broadcaster. However, one unexpected event threatened to shake the very foundations of Nine's success when it discovered its arch rival had secured the rights to the Rugby League football from under its nose. "It was too late, the deal was done, there was nothing we could do." said Chisholm.

"I called a meeting of my senior executives, and we realised we had to do something different. We had to accept that we had lost the rights. What could we do to ensure we kept the audience? That's when the idea came from out of left field: What would keep viewers watching, what loyalty did they have beyond their individual team?" The State of Origin Matches were conceived, and they turned out to be a programming coup. Beyond a person's loyalty to his team, lay his loyalty to his state, and New South Wales and Queensland were age-old Rugby League rivals. The Nine team set about creating a huge league event. In less than a month, they had negotiated, planned, and promoted the sellout matches. Nine kept its number one position.

"The only thing that's certain in the media is change," said Sam. "If you're standing still, you're going backwards! We are currently going through a technological revolution equalled only by the Industrial Revolution at the end of the last century. Businesses need to keep ahead of the trend; they need new software, new reasons to buy.

"Things don't suddenly change; there's a fair deal of predictability. You need to know what you are doing step by step, bottom up. As a leader you have to create a scenario where nothing comes out of the blue. The person who wins is the person who makes the least mistakes. Try to reduce the error factor.

"Hire people who are smarter than you. You should be the conductor of the orchestra. Let your musicians get on with it. Don't try to play the piano better than your virtuoso. These people have unique skills. Create a winning team, a team of champions."

A former executive, who was one of Sam's direct reports, said to me, "I have never worked for anyone, who was better at delegating and dealing with issues that would have overcome a lesser man." Sam said he was well positioned to delegate and make tough decisions because of "the unfailing support that I always got from Rupert Murdoch."

Delegating is not only just the signing off of assignments to others. It's the delegation of power to others—where employees feel empowered to bring ideas forth and are unafraid to fail with them. "If you give somebody something to do, people don't always get it right. And one of the things you've got to do when you're working with people is, you've got to be prepared to support them if they're wrong. You shouldn't lose faith in them. Everyone makes mistakes."

However, delegation does not mean relinquishing responsibility. "When you are the boss, the buck stops with you," he said. When delegating or getting ready for the unexpected, every executive needs to be at the ready, even accepting that she is going to have to face some insecurity at the top. "If you fail, you'll probably be sacked and lose your share options. The biggest thing to conquer is your own insecurity. You know, when you are a CEO, it's pretty lonely.

You have a responsibility. People rely on you to make the company work and grow. You're the person who has to deliver on it. It's not something to take lightly," he added. "It's very nice when everything's roaring along . . . but it's a high-risk business being the boss. Insecurity's a factor, it's a constant."

At this time in his life, Sam sees media as a "spectator sport." When he's not on his ranch or walking his beloved dog Wilson with his wife, Sue, he's involved in philanthropic pursuits. Sam was appointed by former prime minister Kevin Rudd to chair the Australian Organ and Transplant Advisory Authority, and he is also chair of the Chris O'Brien Lifehouse—a center of excellence for Australian Cancer research and treatment. Running a not-for-profit organization needs a different approach. "Like a general, you can't pick your team, but unlike in business, where most people are concerned with their self-interest, everyone in the not-for-profit world is involved because they want to do good. The challenge is to harness that goodwill and create a strong team," he said. "As the chair, I'm there to guide and support the chief executive and the board."

Lastly, Sam said he has learned to expect the unexpected: not everything works out as promised or planned. "There are so many imponderables," he said. The thing is to not spend all your time having post mortems on what didn't work but, rather, "concentrate on what does work."

10

LAYING
IT *on the* LINE

MARCH 2008

THE THOUGHT THAT the expedition could be ruined after so much preparation and excitement was pure torment. It was tearing me apart. Unless we had full and complete backing from the Enham board, I might be forced to cancel and tell the members of my team that I'd failed them. All that planning would have been in vain.

However, I wasn't going down without a fight. Hans calmly reminded me of something that I had always said before negotiations: be prepared to walk away. You can't hold an enterprise together just by sheer force of personality. This was just what I needed to hear. As usual, Hans reminded me of the perfect thing when I needed to hear it most.

But I was edgy. After so many months of setbacks and ambiguity, our project was in a state of constant threat. We couldn't maneuver freely because, at any moment, Enham might pull the rug out from under us. We were cornered. I was going to have to force a decision from my critics.

It was already clear that the trustees' main balking point was cost. It seemed that in their view, from the outside looking in, our project was potentially using huge chunks of charity money for nothing but a self-indulgent frolic. To them, it surely seemed as though our mission did not offer any significant value. I had to convince the people on the Enham board that there was a significant benefit from what we were doing.

I decided to address the money issue head on by writing a letter to both the chairman and the CEO of Enham, reviewing the original vision and how and why it fit so perfectly with Enham's mission of unleashing potential. Then I proved my commitment. I told them that Hans and I would pay for the documentary. If the proceeds didn't cover Enham's outlay, we'd cover the shortfall. That way, Enham would have some upside if the film were a hit. If it wasn't, Enham would remain safe, never risking being out of pocket. It was a bold and expensive step, but there was no other way.

Then I spelled it out as clearly as I could: either they should fight as one with me to ensure the success of this project, or they should just abandon it now. It was that simple. I waited for a response and tried to manage my emotions.

The call came as Hans and I were driving down the autobahn in Germany toward the Frankfurt airport. The board of trustees had passed the proposal.

Looking at the situation afterward, I saw what had worked. I had laid it on the line objectively, I had made it clear that I was willing to walk away, and, most important, I had directly addressed the issue that concerned them most: cost. It was an important lesson.

Even with renewed board approval, we couldn't afford to relax. Now we had to take another close, hard look at our overall strategy and carefully fine-tune it, looking for last-minute improvements. When I looked at this project, I spotted two key improvements that we needed to make.

The first was that this trip should have global appeal. As it happened, just a few months before we were set to go up the mountain, I was attending a meeting of the Harvard Women's Leadership Board. There I met Maha Al Juffali. She is *the* voice for disability advocates in Saudi Arabia. It was really remarkable that we had ended up where we had. She and I were sitting in a café in Boston, switching between German and English, she having flown in from Jeddah, Saudi Arabia, and I from London, England, and talking about a climb that would take place in Tanzania. When I told her about the Enham-backed project to climb Kilimanjaro, her eyes lit up with enthusiasm. Within hours, she had produced two new members for our team: Ahmed Afranji, a Saudi Paralympic athlete, and his Lebanese sports teacher, Ali Jaafar. With them, we now had a genuinely international team, with members from the United Kingdom, the United States, Australia, Canada, Lebanon, and Saudi Arabia!

The second very important improvement had to do with altitude sickness. Based on what I'd seen on Mount Meru, this problem still bothered me. We now had 26 people in our climbing party, but only one doctor, Chris Parsons. Chris is an extremely capable surgeon, but he is not a specialist in mountain or adventure sports medicine. As great and invaluable as Chris was, I knew that we needed more than one doctor for the group. As it happened, I was chairing a health conference and had recently met a doctor, Jack Kreindler. He turned out to be a trained mountain medic with a keen interest in sports performance. I told him the idea behind the trek, and he loved it immediately, even pledging to bring a second mountain medic with him, Laura Jackson, who runs mountain marathons as a hobby!

Safety had always been my biggest worry, and suddenly we had not one but two of the world's leading experts in acute mountain sickness.

Now we were rolling. Everything was humming along. As I checked items off the list, I saw the dream slowly forming into reality. This was really going to happen! The long-awaited opportunity was materializing as surely as the Rose Glow. The list of remaining challenges was shrinking fast, it seemed, and soon the entire team would be meeting at London's Heathrow Airport.

LEADERSHIP LESSON NO. 10: DECISIONS

As the old song by Kenny Rogers advises, you have to know when to hold your cards, know when to fold them, and know when to walk away from the game.

This is great gambling advice that is hard to follow when you're on either a winning or a losing streak. There is always the feeling (you know it if you've ever been to a casino) that maybe that next round of play will turn the situation around in your favor or that your lucky streak will last yet another hand. The city of Las Vegas was built on dumb bets like this. People rarely know when to walk away.

In business, knowing when to walk away is key—whether it means deciding against an acquisition that on paper would create significant synergies, saying no to a deal when the price is becoming unreasonable, leaving a toxic workplace, or simply leaving for a better atmosphere altogether. The true leader needs to be prepared to walk away and knows when to do so. It is a must-have skill. To walk or not to walk? For the most part, you can go with your gut instincts. But there are other signs you can look for that aren't as obvious, signs that provide a serious signal of when to walk away.

Here are a few of them that I've observed during my career. Is your company playing musical chairs at the CEO level or with other C-level positions? That's a sign of either a contentious board of directors or nearly impossible expectations. The opposite can also be a warning sign: Is the existing management too entrenched? Has the CEO been in that position for decades without proper succession planning?

Has your company been trying to raise money and failing, either in a friends-and-family syndicate round or at a private equity/venture capital level? It could be the CEO's lack of vision or presentation skills. It may also be that the idea is simply not bankable. Even Twitter, a company that survived for years with no revenue model whatsoever and was based on the then seemingly insane idea of 140-character updates, could raise money. Boy CEO Mark Zuckerberg raised large amounts of capital for Facebook, which in its first iteration was pretty lackluster.

Are customers responding? If all you hear is a virtual dial tone when you reach out, if there's no viral excitement happening on social media sites, or if customer feedback is a dead zone, then your warning lights should go on. This is not to say that it's always wise to walk away from a failing endeavor, especially if you have the clout or the position to examine the problem and fix it. In that case, not walking away might be an incredible career step. That is probably why Michael Korda advised, "Never walk away from failure. On the contrary, study it carefully and imaginatively for its hidden assets." Try to turn the situation around, and if you do decide to walk away at a later stage, do so from a position of strength.

KNOW WHEN TO WALK AWAY

Knowing when to walk away is something that's easier said than done. Examine your circumstances. Are you in a no-win situation? Is the effort more trouble than it's worth, or is it rife with troublesome, toxic personalities? Is the price too high for a position you want to keep or a company you want to acquire? Think long and hard about it. Don't walk away lightly. But there are times when you must close the door behind you. Knowing when to walk away is an essential skill of a true leader.

Walking away should never be a rash decision. Loyalty is important, and leaving a company for greener pastures should not be taken lightly. One significant study of career histories looked at the CEOs of *Financial Times* top 500

European companies and Standard & Poor's top 500 U.S. firms. This study showed that 25 percent of them had been with the same company throughout their careers. My friend Marty Wickstrom became president of Nordstrom's after 19 years with the company. Staying power is often rewarded, but it needs to be balanced.

Your strongest negotiating position, as every car buyer probably knows, is being willing to walk away from a deal that is best refused. The genius behind the *Peanuts* cartoon series, Charles Schultz, once said, "No problem is so formidable that you can't walk away from it." However, don't walk away from a deal, a company, or a project because of personality clashes. So often I see people giving up because they cannot get along with somebody. That is not an appropriate reason, unless it is a matter of principle. Try to put yourself in the other person's shoes, find common ground, and understand his concerns.

Sometimes the fight is not worth it. As a young lawyer, I was subjected to sexual harassment. The senior partner who managed the clients whose accounts I really wanted to work on was more interested in having an affair with me than in having me on the team, and when I refused, he decided not to give me any work. I could have sued the firm, but I decided that the cost was too high.

Successful leaders have an uncanny ability to choose the type and the timing of their battles carefully. If you decide to walk away, do so under the following circumstances:

▸ After you have tried everything in your power to change the situation

- ▶ When it is a matter of principle

- ▶ After you have stopped to learn from and properly reflected on the situation

- ▶ When you have chosen the timing so as to give yourself the best possible step up

- ▶ When the possible downside consequences do not justify continuing

- ▶ When you have given consideration to what comes next and to how a subsequent battle could be won

- ▶ When you are leaving from a position of strength

Walking away from a situation is stressful at the best of times. Going through the checklist above can make your departure easier and can achieve the intended result.

▶ *In conversation with* ◀
MINISTER MOHAMED LOTFI MANSOUR

Mohamed Mansour, chairman of Mansour Group and Egypt's former minister for transport, has been part of the Egyptian political and business elite for decades. If you meet his friends and acquaintances, you'll find yourself among some of the most influential figures in the North African region. Still, he knows better than most what it is like to be caught up in difficult circumstances, where none of the available options are easy ones.

At the time of this writing, uncertainty looms large over Egypt; Mohamed's GM dealerships there are closed, and his McDonald's franchises have been looted and burned.

This certainly is not the first setback in the life of this successful entrepreneur and former government minister. "I grew up in a well-to-do family," he told me. "My father had the second-largest cotton-exporting company in Egypt, and at that time, that was back in the 1950s, cotton was the main export of the country." During his elementary school years, Egypt was a British colony with a very good education system for those who could afford it. A very athletic boy, Mohamed loved sports.

But his life took a sudden tragic and dramatic turn. When he was only 10 years old, he was the victim of a terrible auto accident. As a result, he found himself confined to a hospital bed and unable to live the normal, active life of a teenage boy.

"I was one of the good soccer players, in the position of center forward. I broke records in swimming, and in track and field . . . so sport was a big thing in my life until the summer of 1958, when I had just turned 10. There was a serious accident. A car crashed into me and completely broke my leg." The accident was so severe that the surgeon recommended that the leg be amputated, but Mohamed had a different idea and refused to give his consent. "I said 'no,' and that was at the age of 10. . . . I was determined at that time to keep my leg." Luckily, says Mohamed, doctors managed to treat the infection. "I stayed in a cast in bed for three years, where I couldn't even sleep on my side; I remember that I would sleep sitting up," he recalled, with his eyes gazing past me and into the distance.

As a result of his circumstances, he became an avid reader, informing himself about everything that was going on around him. And he found himself spending more time with his father than he had normally done when he was active in sports. He told me that those years he spent confined to a hospital bed "made me the man I am today. . . . This was a very big learning experience for me to learn about values, to learn about business, to learn about life, to talk about politics. When one is young, these things go into your brain and they form you, the man you will become."

This period of confinement also gave him a real sympathy for the challenges faced by the disabled and the disadvantaged. As a result of all his experience with his accident, the adult Mohamed has founded, chaired, and been involved with multiple charities that aim to improve the quality of life for others.

Mohamed has found himself in other challenging situations. The Nasser revolution took away the family fortune, but his father made sure that his three sons were able to leave Egypt. Mohamed studied in the United States. However, a university education was possible only through his willingness to work as a busboy and dishwasher. "This experience steeled me and shaped me more than anything else."

Since the Nasser revolution, by building on a firm foundation, he remained even and balanced during his heady days as minister of transport of Egypt, where he was responsible for 285,000 employees.

"I was asked to join the Egyptian government and became the minister of transport. I had the big responsibility of rebuilding the transport system. It includes the roads, the bridges, the railroad—the second-oldest railroad in the world—it includes the underground, the ports, and the night transport. We were transporting four million people a day, four million."

After four years, he resigned from the government following a railroad accident that resulted in several fatalities. His resignation is very unusual in developing countries. Why would he resign? I knew from talking to him that here was a real fighter, a man with fierce determination to reach a goal, someone who had overcome incredible odds and does not walk away lightly.

"When you have this determination and you have values, you always do what you think is right. I think this is very important because I would never walk away if I felt that a friend needed me."

But this time it was different. "An accident happened in which 18 people died," he told me as if it had happened yesterday. "A cow was crossing, a train hit the cow, the train stopped, another train coming from behind crashed into it, and some of the people sitting in the back carriage died, some of them were injured." But why resign? Surely accidents happen, and the minister of transport was not driving the train.

"I felt at the time that it took real courage to walk away," he said. "Egyptian ministers do not resign; either they are sacked or they die in their seat. . . . I went to the prime minister, and I told him that I felt it was time for me to leave."

Mohamed chose to take the radical step of resigning for several reasons. He told me, "I felt that I had to set an example—in a country like Egypt, with 7,000 years of history, there had to be someone who was willing to take responsibility." Second, he had given four years to his country and was satisfied with what he had achieved. Third, the media in Egypt had become hostile, and it was a matter of deciding what was best for his family. "I'm very close to my family," he said quietly. "I could see the pain in my son's face." His family could not understand why the government-controlled press coverage was so negative. Where was the support, the fairness? His son's incredulity was like a dagger in his father's heart when he wondered aloud: "Does the minister drive the train? Does the minister himself stand in the crossing and open and close the crossing? How could they do this to you, dad?" The public scrutiny and attack on his name was a significant factor in his decision. "I value my name; it's so important."

What advice does Mohamed Mansour have for people who are considering making a change? Have courage, clear-sightedness, and an ability to examine your priorities. "It takes courage, whether you are in government, whether it be in the private sector, to be able to say, 'I need to move on.'" You must move on, however, if "the challenge is no longer there—I think challenge is the fuel, it's the energy that makes a true person want to achieve something. If the challenge is no longer there in a particular situation, move on, have the confidence to move on and try something else, and create an example for others."

As you can see, the removal of Hosni Mubarak was not the first time that Mohamed had found himself on the wrong side of circumstances, but he remains optimistic about his country's future in spite of its significant current difficulties.

"This country will have a future"; he is certain. And so does each one of us, he exhorts us to remember. One "human being can really do a lot, whether he's in Africa, whether he's in Australia, whether he's in Timbuktu or whatever. It takes a fighter; one has got to fight in his life and to fight from the standpoints of value and integrity. That may include leaving a particular position, but things do work out okay."

An optimistic attitude, openness to change, and the willingness to fight for one's values: those are the keys to Mohamed's phenomenal ability to deal with change.

11

A FINAL HURDLE

JUNE 2008

WE WERE LESS THAN two weeks away from leaving for Africa. Just as I thought that I had dealt with the last obstacle, another one appeared out of nowhere. Some colleagues of Dr. Jack Kreindler, the doctor who was coming on the trip with us, had something to say about the matter. One of them wrote me a letter that was packed with searing criticism. He strongly advised us that the trip was too dangerous, and that someone could get seriously hurt. He suggested that we either cancel the expedition or factor in extra time and extend it.

At first, the letter seemed to present a terrible dilemma. The fact was, we could not afford to add any more days to the climb. We had already allowed for extra time to acclimatize, and we simply didn't have the financial resources to add more days to our itinerary. And I felt safe with the advice of my experts, Steve Ballantyne and the professionals at Alpine Ascents. We had built up incredible, unstoppable momentum, and we were now fully prepared for the climb. Yet here was this letter in my hands, counseling us to abandon almost two years' worth of planning and struggle. Suddenly it seemed as if I would have blood on my hands if I did not drastically change or abandon the expedition.

With a cold, sinking feeling, I decided to call Jack and ask for his opinion. What if the letter was really his idea? My fingers actually shook as I dialed his number. When he answered, I asked him point-blank if he knew of the letter and if he was involved in any way.

Jack took his time answering. But to my relief, he was still squarely behind the project.

"Look, I admit it's controversial," he said. "The big issue is really the last day's climb." He reminded me that, to allow the human body time to acclimatize, the ideal vertical climbing distance per day is 500 meters. We were planning to take the mountain gently throughout most of the climb, but of necessity, our plans had us making a final 1,000-meter trek to the summit—a rapid, make-or-break blitz to the peak.

"And that's the reason we're taking three medics," Jack said firmly, reminding me that we were offering close medical supervision. "The minute anyone shows signs of altitude sickness, we can take action. If that means sending them and their buddy back down, so be it." No one would be allowed to ascend higher than safety dictated. And of course, we'd been stressing to every team member from the start that actually making it to the summit was not the be-all and end-all of the journey.

So Jack was still committed. The team was still in place. I ignored the letter.

LEADERSHIP LESSON NO. 11: CRITICISM

Some of us have a hard time dealing with criticism. We want everyone to like us and what we do. Even a hint of criticism is enough to drive us into the depths of despair. The problem is simple: we are taking the criticism too personally; we are treating it as an attack on our identity. This is understandable, because very few people are fortunate enough to have had parents who clearly differentiated between the child and the acts committed by the child that were the object of the parents' disapproval—in other words, who rebuked the action without condemning the actor. Doing otherwise can breed deep insecurities and low self-esteem.

As you rise through the ranks and become more visible in your organization, the amount of criticism you receive will increase—some of it is constructive, some of it negative or just plain malicious. There will be people who are envious of your skills and your rise into the leadership ranks, and odds are that someone will try to tear you down with unwarranted criticism, either to your face or behind your back. The most painful criticism is that in which your integrity is questioned and your motives are misunderstood by the very people who should and probably do know better. This is a reality of business. You need to learn how to deal with both your enemies and your "frenemies."

During my investment banking days, my team and I had just closed a multimillion-dollar structured finance transaction, and I was expecting appropriate recognition from my boss. Instead, he went out of his way to diminish our accomplishment, and when I voiced my concern about his behavior, he barked, "Take it like a man!" When I mentioned the incident to my husband, he texted me back the following: "Some days you are the pigeon, some days the statue. Just live with it." Crude, I thought, but how true.

Dealing with constructive and unfair criticism wisely and calmly is essential to both your mental health and your success. Researchers Jay Knippen and Thad Green, writing for a psychological journal on workplace learning, have studied deeply on the topic of criticism and ways in which a successful person needs to deal with it.

DEAL WISELY WITH CRITICISM

If you work at a yes-man company where criticism is rare, be brave and ask for it from those whom you manage or lead and those whom you report to. Ask what you can be doing better. In my opinion, proactive behavior of this type is the best way to manage criticism—find it before it finds you. But when it does find you—and it will—deal with it wisely. Evaluate the person who is providing the "feedback." Ignore anonymous comments, no matter how outrageous they may be. How you deal with criticism will say a lot about you in terms of your character, confidence, and willingness to learn.

Handling criticism wisely is a five-step process, Knippen and Green say. The five steps are

- Prepare yourself, because it is likely that criticism will eventually land on you.

- Accept the criticism when you hear it without being defensive or responding in a personally hurt or angry way.

- Try to understand the criticism—ask questions and really get a handle on what the criticism entails.

- Reach agreement with the critic, especially if you report to this person, on ways in which you can change what's being criticized.

- Finally, give positive comments back to the critic, which will reinforce the idea that you are the kind of leader who can handle criticism and use it as a catalyst for change.

Many studies over the years have shown that women are more likely than men to take criticism personally and respond in a distressed way. A possible explanation for this is sports: men who spend their boyhoods being yelled at by coaches and fellow teammates eventually learn that criticism is all part of the game. Women, who don't grow up in similar environments, may have a harder time realizing this. Regardless of your gender, your goals and your career path are too important for you to risk getting a reputation as a thin-skinned, difficult employee who is unwilling to learn from criticism, even if it is delivered in an unpleasant manner.

Try to remember that, as Malcolm X once said, "If you have no critics, you'll likely have no success." Criticism, like setbacks and repeated failures, is perhaps unpleasant, but it's a necessary ingredient in a successful climb to the top. CEOs, who report to a board of directors and have people reporting to them as well, learn this quickly. If they don't learn it, they won't last long.

Whether they are framed as "feedback" or "criticism," the words you hear may sound harsh. Here's a final thought on the subject that's worth emphasizing: guard your facial expressions if the criticism or feedback is overtly nasty or negative. The point is that you are willing to learn from it, so you should remain calm and collected.

The other side of the coin is equally important. As a leader, you will find yourself in situations where you have to provide criticism. Do it in private, and make sure that it's constructive. Do not bruise your employees or colleagues unnecessarily. Words are incredibly powerful, and they should be filtered carefully. One sage said: your words should pass through three gates: (1) truth, (2) necessity, and (3) kindness. You can get much more innovation and productivity from your team if you create a safe environment in which criticism is coupled with praise and in which actions, rather than the person, are corrected.

▶ *In conversation with* ◀
KARIN FORSEKE

Dealing wisely with criticism isn't just good practice, it's a necessity for all leaders who want to maintain their sanity, equilibrium, and confidence on the way to the top and at the top. Karin Forseke, formerly the CEO of D. Carnegie & Co., a Nordic investment bank listed on the Stockholm Stock Exchange, is no stranger to criticism. She's also an expert at taking it gracefully and issuing it kindly.

As senior advisor to the Swedish minister of financial markets and local government, Karin was responsible for the privatization of half a dozen companies with a market value totaling $20 billion. Ranked among the 100 most influential people in capital markets by *Financial News*, Karin is a good friend, one whom I admire deeply, particularly as I saw the way she handled some of the most brutal media attacks. An incredibly thoughtful person, she is very well qualified to talk about the all-important issue of criticism.

Constructive criticism, as opposed to anonymous or personal attacks that are intended to assassinate the character of a leader, is the only worthwhile criticism, said Karin. "Constructive criticism never takes place publicly. Public criticism is never constructive. But constructive criticism can be productive. This is criticism that you present with an alternative outcome. Instead of saying, 'You are wrong; this is wrong,' it is about saying, 'Yes, that's one way of looking at it, but have you considered this other way?'"

How can you determine whether the criticism you provide is constructive? It's easy, she said. "It is how it is presented. It is not constructive if it is presented in anger, or in a huff, or in an unfriendly environment as a put-down. It must be presented with the intention that the criticism is actually trying to further the debate, not an attack."

Personal attacks, she said, are always to be avoided. They throw team members or employees into a corner, forcing them to defend themselves instead of figuring out a way to actually listen to the content of the critical commentary and react positively to it in a way that benefits everyone.

Dealing with criticism—not doling it out but actually receiving it from above or from colleagues, competitors, the press, or anonymous voices on the Internet—she added, is something that every leader needs to become expert at.

"The important thing with criticism, particularly with public attacks or even personal attacks, is to take a deep breath, listen to one's self, and listen to one's own reactions. Actually think about, 'Why am I reacting so strongly to this? Why am I so hurt and upset by this?' Analyzing one's reactions to criticism can provide a good hint as to its validity and whether to take it seriously. After all, when you are a leader, there are petty jealousies, enemies, and people who criticize out of their own personal weaknesses and feelings of being threatened. It is important to distinguish such criticism from criticism that actually calls your attention to something that you could be doing better.

"I think the more serious you feel about a criticism, the more it hits a raw nerve—or it's attacked your integrity somehow," she said. "The more painful the criticism feels or the more anguish it causes, the more time you should take to try to find out why it makes you react this way. Because that's how you can learn from yourself. That's one extreme. Another time to be concerned about yourself is when you get criticism and you seriously think that everybody else is wrong and you are right. That's a red flag. It might be a hint that you've been at the summit too long."

In her own experience, Karin took a public bashing in the press when she decided not to issue bonuses to some employees who had taken a threatening tone during negotiations. Karin decided to let them walk. "I decided that these were unreasonable demands and . . . their behaviors did not support the values I wanted the organization to represent." At least one major business publication, though, took up the issue with an article that was broadly critical of Karin, "claiming that the new CEO does not understand how important bonuses are in the financial industry."

"Now, I read that article, and I thought, that is very sad. But it did not hurt me. I did not feel angry. I didn't have a negative reaction," Karin pointed out, reflecting that when a leader knows intuitively that criticism is wrongly placed, the wisest way to deal with it is to follow one's own course and listen to one's intuition. "When you are really aligned between your values and your actions, then criticism doesn't hurt so much. Of course, it doesn't feel nice. But it doesn't tear you apart. It is just another brick in building your experience, giving you the confidence to take a bigger step next time."

Dealing wisely with criticism—being able to ignore the anonymous hordes on social media and to listen to your own gut and analyze your actions as they compare to the criticism—is a learning process that an executive endures over time. As for the article that questioned Karin's ability to understand her own business, "that was fuel on the fire to some people who were also inclined to think they deserved more bonus, and ammunition for others who felt that being loud should not be rewarded. But on the other hand, it actually solidifies you, and you become confident in your own values."

Karin worries about the rise of social media, "where all of a sudden people can critique you without taking responsibility for their critique. They can throw it out in the world of social media anonymously and make horrendous attacks on people without basically having any fundamental knowledge." This can damage people, but one must remember the source. Social media are, after all, "a completely different ball game. There is just so much data out there." The question that a leader must ask, she said, is, "How do we actually learn to distill what is valuable, and how do we learn to just ignore and jettison what is rubbish?" That is the challenge for leaders coming up in business today, she said.

It is interesting to note that when Karin took the CEO post at D. Carnegie, she was among the first female CEOs of a publicly listed investment bank. This put her on a pedestal, for a time. But being on a pedestal, of course, meant that there were those who wanted to throw her off. The important thing, she said, is to believe in yourself.

"One thing I've learned," Karin said, "is that you're never as good as they say you are when you're at the top of the pedestal." And you are never as bad, she added, as critics say you are when they are trying to throw you off.

Karin's advice is to keep your moorings, stay true to your values, and follow your instincts. This always helps when you analyze whether the criticism you receive is worth taking. It's important to listen to it, though, and to your own reaction to it. "Go through it. It's worth it. You come out stronger." Over time, Karin found that dealing wisely with criticism became second nature. Make it yours, too.

12

To AFRICA!

THE DAY OF OUR DEPARTURE finally arrived. At Heathrow, I waited to meet up with our climbers, who were flying in from all over the world. Some of them would be meeting one another for the first time, and it was the first time that all of the team had been assembled together. The excitement was contagious.

I just hoped that the film crew would be in place to capture this early part of our journey. I watched the expression on James Bridges's face. He looked exultant—he'd never been on a plane before. Liz Curtis, who had been trapped in her house for years, hadn't been in an airport since she was a child. Alex Adams was busy buying hundreds of cigarettes at the duty-free shop. I couldn't help but laugh as Alex tried to strip all of us of our duty-free allowances so that he could hoard cigarettes for a climb up the world's largest freestanding mountain.

The plan was to fly from London to Nairobi, Kenya. There, officials would hold a plane for us, which would take us to Arusha, Tanzania. The schedule was extremely tight. I was worried a bit by a delay in our initial takeoff, but before we knew it, we were heading down the runway at Heathrow, on our way up and out of London. And to Africa! I watched the grinning face of our autistic climber, James Smith. He was staring at the in-flight video screen map that showed our flight south over Europe and the Mediterranean.

We seemed to be making good time. I was a frequent flyer and was quite familiar with the logistics of connecting flights. Surely they would hold the plane for us in Nairobi, but what about our luggage? Could our gear be left behind in Nairobi if we had to make such a rapid turnaround onto the next flight?

We disembarked in Nairobi, and I made sure to speak with the official who was responsible for luggage transfers. Everything was being filmed, I remarked pointedly, and if Kenya Airlines got our luggage with us to Arusha, that would make the airline look its best. Desperate to make sure that our luggage and our expensive film gear would not be left unattended somewhere on the airstrip or airport, I shadowed this official until he confirmed beyond a doubt that all the film equipment was safely on board.

I dashed onto the waiting plane with Hans. Ali and Ahmed, our Saudi climbers, were already on board and were looking for me. I raced to meet them face-to-face for the first time. Ahmed, who has cerebral palsy and learning difficulties, was a lean-faced, gangly young man with a serious expression. Ahmed's father had died only weeks before, and Ahmed was making this climb in his memory. Ali, Ahmed's sports coach, was heavier, with twinkling, warm brown eyes and a jolly expression. Now I had met everyone involved with the expedition. Finally, the whole group was intact. My heart lifted with thoughts of what we were soon to accomplish. We were all in the small plane, cramped together, and we hadn't even had time to make proper introductions.

I finally introduced our Saudi climbers to the rest of the team when we landed at Arusha. It was two o'clock in the morning. We trooped together from the airport building into the warm African night. Everyone had made it safe and sound. As promised, even the film gear made it. Then I saw that about half of our other baggage was nowhere to be found. Hans and I had only our hand luggage, and many of us were missing equipment.

"Er, Herta, " Gordon, our cinematographer, said, catching my eye. "I think we have another problem besides the luggage." I noticed a large man in uniform glowering at us.

The man turned out to be from the Tanzanian immigration authorities. There was an issue regarding our film permit. According to him, our paperwork (obtained from and processed by the Tanzanian High Commission in London) wasn't actually a permit at all; it was merely a permission slip for a permit. Now the immigration authorities were threatening to impound all our film equipment until the correct files and forms had been completed.

Here we were in Africa, with no climbing equipment and no right to film. It was practically beyond belief. Fighting disenchantment, I snapped into reality mode. There was nothing I could have done to prevent this, but now we needed a quick and positive outcome. Any lengthy holdup would force us to cancel the entire expedition. We didn't have the luxury of patiently waiting days to get this whole thing figured out. There was nothing to be done that night. We went to the hotel, and I went to bed, filled with despair.

The next morning, a Sunday, our team reassembled, and I saw how strong we were. Steve set off to the airport to see about our missing luggage, while John Hauf, the lead guide from AAI, gave us a calming and sensible briefing. Yes, it was clear that we had to move the next day, but he was unruffled. John had been up Kilimanjaro 26 times—he was no stranger to these parts. He told us that AAI would plunder its own stock for equipment if necessary. I had deep faith that we could not have come this far and negotiated so many obstacles, all for nothing.

My mobile phone rang at 12:30. It was Steve. "They must have found our luggage," I said to Hans. Just before I answered the phone, Hans muttered something about me being a stark raving optimist.

Sure enough, I was soon proven right. Steve confirmed that he had recovered the luggage. Only the bag belonging to Ahmed with a drum inside—the drum that Ahmed had hoped would keep our spirits high during the climb—was still missing.

As for the film permit, we were in hot water. Monday was a Tanzanian bank holiday, and that was the day we had to begin our climb. We couldn't go up without cameras and sound equipment. The whole sponsorship depended on this documentary film that we'd planned.

Again, John Hauf came to the rescue. What a stark contrast he was to the first expedition guide we had had on

Kilimanjaro! We asked John if he knew a local fixer for our problem, and he did. His contact managed to get through to someone at the Ministry of Tourism and arrange an appointment for Tuesday morning in the capital, Dar es Salaam. Meanwhile, we began discussions to see if there was any way to salvage the situation and begin filming the beginning of the climb, despite our lack of a permit. It wasn't smooth sailing (at one point the ministry wanted to impound our film crew along with the equipment), but at last the Tanzanians agreed that the crew could use handheld cameras until the permit came through on Tuesday. Once our fixer had the film permit in hand, he would call us on the satellite phones we were carrying on the mountain, and the crew could pop open the cases with the larger cameras.

Our problem was solved. In the process, and quite unintentionally, we'd managed to turn a major problem into an advantage. As the cameramen later explained to me, the larger cameras on tripods and cranes were perfect for sweeping, wide shots, but those shots would capture vistas that would be available to us only after we were further up the mountain. The handheld cameras would give the early footage a gritty quality and be better at getting close-ups. The whole first day, we would be climbing through the rainforest anyway. The little cameras were perfect for registering our emotions and establishing personalities and relationships early on, from the climbers to the doctors and everyone in between. The film produced this way would feel more intense and look more dramatic.

I had to smile to myself in the hotel lobby as I watched Gordon popping a cassette into his camera, demonstrating why this would be so much easier the first day. I had to learn to stop trying to be Superwoman. It was important that I stay calm and not be ashamed to ask for help. This was surely the ticket.

Finally, on Monday morning, we all piled into Toyota Land Cruisers and set out, euphoric once more. We bounced along the dusty road, with Kilimanjaro looming before us— to me it seemed at once both beautiful and menacing. Irresistible. I nudged Hans and pointed to the sky. To our utter relief, the weather was perfect. There wasn't a cloud in sight. The Land Cruisers turned off the main road and began jolting over a rutted track through the bush. In front of us, I could see the arch of the Machame Gate. Named after a nearby village, the gate announced the entrance to a trail that would give our team the opportunity to experience one of the most remarkable places on Earth.

Now, we would start the climb.

LEADERSHIP LESSON NO. 12: THE EGO

Egocentric leadership is one of the most lethal influences in business, politics, churches, and every other walk of life. The point is, it is not all about you. It really isn't. Sometimes it feels as if it is. Throughout this book, you've learned about the skills that you need to master in order to make it to the top of your organization or reach your highest goals. But really, it is not about you.

The mission is always more important than ego. Most of the time, you need to set your ego aside and shelve it. If your ego is healthy and you have a strong sense of identity, you will have the discipline to keep your ego under control. Most of the time, interesting, high-capacity people have big egos. Placing the mission before your ego not only will get you to your goals more quickly but also will put things in perspective and set an example for your team. Let your team members know that you and your ego are not the center of the universe. Neither is any single member of the team. The mission comes first, and that is what you and your team are out to accomplish.

As of the writing of this book, the Egyptian people have succeeded in peacefully forcing the resignation of President Hosni Mubarak, who occupied the highest political office in that country for more than 30 years. Every time American diplomats exerted pressure on him to step aside or to bring about political reform, he would claim that his presence was essential to avoid a takeover by Islamic fundamentalists. His claim was that he, Mubarak, was the only person who could keep Egypt safe. My numerous visits to Cairo and my interactions with Egypt's elite made it clear to me that Mubarak cared first and foremost about himself. (Even the stripes in his custom-made $10,000 suits spelled his name, "Hosni.") He believed that he was truly irreplaceable.

What is true for politicians is, too often, true for businesspeople as well. When they are faced with the choice of what's best for the project and what makes them look good, they will choose the latter. Such egocentric behavior isn't teamwork, it isn't excellence, and sooner or later it will hinder your chances of achieving your goal.

ALWAYS PLACE MISSION BEFORE EGO

Ask yourself which is really important: the mission or your ego? It is not true that everything revolves around you and your success. If you make it do so, you'll be setting a destructive example for your team. Be clear about your vision, place your mission first, and watch out for egos—yours and those of the others on your team. Uncontrolled egos can cause the best teams to fail.

Some of the megamergers in the banking industry have had nothing to do with creating more efficient, more profitable organizations. Rather, they were driven by the unfettered egos of the CEOs. Ego appears to have been the impetus behind Citibank's merger with Travelers and behind the Royal Bank of Scotland's purchase of ABN Amro at a ridiculously inflated price. Once very healthy, strong banks, they ended up on the brink of collapse and needed to be bailed out by their respective governments.

There are so many reasons why acting from a self-centered perspective is detrimental to your rise to the top (or will bring about your precipitous fall once you have reached it) that there is no space to list them all here. Egocentric employees, managers, and leaders are naturally unable to follow the necessary rules for leadership success that I've detailed previously. They can't handle criticism. They dwell on failure or cover it up. They are more concerned about themselves than about the team around them.

You need to learn to be mission-centered rather than self-centered. In western society, where children are reared from the earliest age to believe that they are all winners regardless of the number of points won, where they get trophies just for participating in group sports or hobbies, the number of self-centered employees who may even be blind to the company's overall mission or its goals is bound to increase. This is not acceptable.

Does your company have a mission statement? Do you have a personal mission statement? If not, then set to work creating both. Your personal mission statement should, of course, reflect the mission of the organization. They should be aligned. That is a good test of whether you are overly ego-centered.

Train those around you—your team and any other employees whom you affect by example—to think similarly. Everyone at a winning organization, including you, needs to be able to admit mistakes as soon as she realizes them, so that corrective action is possible. Everyone—especially you—needs to know that success primarily relies on everyone working on the same mission—rowing the same boat in the same direction, so to speak. This is the authentic path toward leadership.

Andrew Cohen, author of *Transcending Ego: An Attainable Goal*, speaks directly to that authenticity—the ability to know the difference between your ego's desires and the greater goal that you are serving. "The authentic self," he wrote, "is the best part of a human being. It's the part of you that already cares, that is already passionate. When your authentic self miraculously awakens and becomes stronger than your ego, you will truly begin to make a difference in this world.

You will literally enter into a partnership with the creative principle."

Aligning yourself with your mission and not your own ego is a creative act. The leaders who have the most positive impact are very humble and gracious. They understand their calling and know that they are not indispensable. They fulfill their purpose and move on. Look around, and you will see that most people are unable to achieve this. It's especially hard for leaders, who, when they rise to the top, find themselves surrounded by yes-men and yes-women. Mohamed Mansour, the former transport minister of Egypt, said to me recently: "I am always very worried about leaders who need an entourage of 20 people around them. It means that their egos are out of control." The trappings of power feed their egos, to the detriment of all. They blind leaders to the reality of what is going on. Remember Thomas Carlyle's words: "Egotism is the source and summary of all faults and miseries." Watch yourself carefully, and choose to subordinate your own ego to the greater mission. We would be wise to listen to the advice of the Apostle Peter in his first book in the Bible: "Don't indulge your ego at the expense of your soul."

▶ *In conversation with* ◀
PRESIDENT AND LIEUTENANT GENERAL SERETSE KHAMA IAN KHAMA

Botswana's president, Ian Khama, is very well positioned to speak about what I consider to be one of the toughest lessons a leader must learn—how to put mission before ego.

Khama comes from a long line of leaders. His full name is Seretse Khama Ian Khama. He is the son of former Botswana president Sir Seretse Khama, and his grandfather was Sekgoma II, the presiding chief of the Bamangwato people. His tribal leadership lineage goes back to Kgosikgolo Sekgoma I, who was the chief of the Bamanwato people in the early nineteenth century.

As leader of a very well-governed African democracy, President Khama spoke to me eloquently about the dangers of egoism and the fatal effects it has on a march toward success. He is a man who walks the talk. Keeping the trappings of high office to a minimum, he mixes with the people he was elected to serve with an amazing frequency.

Getting to the top "in many cases is an ego trip. I find that many leaders succumb to the temptations of office and then start abusing their positions—even using their office to improve their own private circumstances." Referring to uprisings in the Middle East, President Khama pointed out that leaders like Colonel Qaddefi of Libya, who stood up and said that they were the ones responsible for their people, and then in the same breath promised to "show no mercy" to demonstrators, no longer deserved to lead. "These are the people you are there to serve," he told me. "It is just something that is extremely sad." But President Khama not only laments the consequences of egomaniacal leadership but will use whatever means are at his disposal to halt the damage. To that end, Botswana was one of the first African nations to break diplomatic relations with Libya.

But no leader, whether he is a head of state or the leader of a small private enterprise, is immune to the temptation that comes with any position of power. And the risk of power corrupting, or leading one to put one's personal ego before the mission at hand, is tremendous. Making sure that you don't fall prey to it requires vigilance.

"My leadership style is people focused," President Khama told me. "But I try very hard to walk the talk. For example, in a democracy, I feel very strongly that the government should be centered around what people's expectations are." Staying well rooted by meeting regularly with the citizenry, he said, is one way to get a realistic view of the people you're serving and maintain focus on the mission.

"I think it's important to keep checking, going back to people and saying, are we delivering per your expectations? And if we are not, fine, then we have to adjust. This gives people the sense that they're able to talk to the people who are in office—to say to them, "This is maybe what you should be doing differently." Citizens then are in the loop when it comes to the direction in which the country should be heading."

Maintaining an ongoing dialogue with the people you're leading is one method of putting mission before ego. Accountability is another. When people are not held accountable by those they serve (and by regular self-checking), it is all too easy for them to make a mission "all about them" and forget what they're really working for.

"It's human nature, but it boils down to the individual's character and how she interprets her roles," he said. That's the "self-discipline aspect of it. And it doesn't just apply to your work ethic; it's even how you conduct yourself in private."

President Khama said that he has other people assist him with self-checks: "I've said to them, 'If you ever see me becoming a different person, different from how I was, just tap me on the shoulder. Say, remember what you said? Well, I'm telling you now. You're starting to behave like one of those egotistic leaders.' I think that might be the best way," he added. "If you can choose the right person, one who would be prepared to tell it to your face, then you would discover that you've fallen into the trap."

In addition to holding himself accountable, he is concerned that egos can often get in the way of his ministers' delivery or performance. His scorecards have become an important part of his management style. And so his ministers' performance is judged, so that they know that it's not about sitting in a black car with a flag on it; that's not what's important, as used to be the perception. They actually have to work to deliver.

President Khama has expressed very clear views on term limits for politicians and the need for proper checks and balances to avoid the abuse of power. We will share more of these insights in the final chapter.

13

The
CLIMB BEGINS

7 TO 9 JULY 2008

WE STOOD AT THE TRAILHEAD, with the sun blazing down on us. Here at Machame Camp, 3,000 meters above sea level, was where our expedition really began. The start of the trail stood before us, deceptively wide and level before it wound its way up and into the rainforest.

All of us were wearing shorts or light trousers, but I knew that it wouldn't be long before we'd be wrapped in thick fleece, as we climbed above and beyond the Kilimanjaro snowline. Standing there in the sunlight that day, anything seemed possible. It is hard to explain, but I felt a transcendent pleasure as I looked at our team. This really was a labor of love for so many of us, who had given of our time, talent, and treasure to get to this point. What a great start to the journey!

This moment reminded me of another journey many years ago, when I left Communist Romania with my parents. As we flew into Austrian airspace, I felt an incredible sense of freedom; high above the clouds, the sun was shining, and a Higher Power somehow smiled on me.

However, there was no time to go down memory lane. I looked back at the team. The Machame Trail's success rate is only about 35 percent. Two out of three climbers never make the summit. Kilimanjaro is deadly, too: every year, the mountain claims an average of eight lives. I looked at our team of 28 people, wondering how we would fare. Certainly, given that 7 of the team were disabled, our chances seemed less than average. Yet we couldn't be more prepared, I told myself.

As the members of our team took pictures of one another, commemorating this beginning, the question lingered: who would make it, and who would fail it? It was hard to tell. The odds were stacked against James Smith. Skinny and beaming, with a buck-toothed smile, he looked so fragile standing there with his thick eyeglasses. It was clear that his severe learning disabilities might make it hard for him to cope. Did he really understand the painstaking drills that we'd tried to give all the climbers? Fortunately, his buddy, an aspiring Australian actor named Morgan Roy, looked quite capable. Watching Morgan check James's kit for the climb, I could see the strong and growing bond between them.

The other James—James Bridges—looked less frail. But for all his robustness, I knew about his degenerative spine condition and the pain it caused him. His wary expression belied his smile. Alex Adams, with his Asperger's, had a terrible depression to factor in. How would he fare when the clouds and the cold set in? And how was Val Bradshaw going to do? Would her injured leg be strong enough to carry

her up the mountain? Was Liz Curtis emotionally capable
of the challenge after walling herself up for so many years—
could she really sleep under the stars after suffering a nervous breakdown and then her agoraphobia for so long? I
didn't know.

I considered Ahmed's cerebral palsy and the fact that he
spoke no English. His buddy, Ali, had the double job of being translator and helping Ahmed up the slope. Since they
were from Saudi Arabia, the two were not used to the cold,
and I knew it would get very cold. And then there was Jamie
Magee, hiking with the rolling gait of a stroke survivor, his
left side paralyzed; but he was smiling widely nonetheless.
Whenever he saw his buddy, Pauline, he'd yell, "Big Mama!"

And what of Pauline? She was not a thin woman. An Enham employee, she had confided in me before that she was
not sure whether she'd trained hard enough for the climb.
We hadn't started yet, but already her face was shiny in the
heat. Everyone had received the suggested training regime,
but it was up to each of us to take it to heart.

We set off into the rainforest. I found myself next to
Michael Price, who would be composing the music for the
documentary of our expedition. He'd been the lead music editor on the *Lord of the Rings* movie trilogy, and we began talking about the numerous films he had been involved
with. While following the trail gradually upward, I pictured
us as hobbits tackling the slopes of the Misty Mountains.

Several hours passed before the welcome sight of lunch
appeared, laid out for us on a long trestle table. There were
even flowers on it—fake ones, but flowers all the same. It
was going to be grueling enough getting up the mountain,

so the expedition planners had offered what luxuries they could to keep our spirits up. There were 180 porters accompanying our expedition (each of them carrying the 18 kilograms allowed by law), and we even had portable sit-down toilets. I imagine we were the envy of countless other campers, who, after a long ascent that had turned their legs to jelly, had to squat painfully on the ground. Our porters, who were used to this route, were carrying the bulk of our baggage ahead of us. Every night, when we reached camp, the tents were set up, and dinner was cooking. This level of professionalism was the benefit of using a high-end company like AAI; the extra expense was well worth it.

Attention to detail is vital to any enterprise—in business or on the mountain—I'd learned. Comfort and reward keep people motivated. Even during my arguments over finance with Enham, I never felt the temptation to skimp on the amenities. There was no compromise on little luxuries for this journey. When or if morale began to plummet, I knew that the first thing we'd regret was being cheap about things.

We reached our first camp as the sun set. Throughout the day, our team had spread out, which is bound to happen when there are different climbers who are moving at different paces. I'd expected that. But it bothered me that night had already fallen before the last stragglers reached camp that first night. This was supposed to be the easiest part of the trek, mostly on well-trodden trails with few steep ascents. Already, there was a clear demarcation in our party, though. There was the fast group and the slow group. The very last to arrive that first night were Jamie Magee and his buddy, "Big Mama" Pauline.

Pauline, who was the first to admit that she was built for comfort, not speed, was having a rough time. As soon as she reached camp, she dissolved into tears. But it was Jamie, half-paralyzed since his childhood injury, who worried me most. All the climbers had walking poles. But to watch Jamie leaning on his poles, painfully dragging his left foot behind him, was just wrenching. Jamie was the weakest member of the expedition, I knew. That was why we had paired him with two buddies, Pauline and Michael, a physically strong young man. But Michael had arrived well before Pauline and Jamie. When they finally arrived, two guides were practically carrying Jamie over the steeper sections of the trail.

Jamie's brother Bryan was also on the expedition, but he was paired with James Bridges. I could see that Bryan was worried and torn about his brother. The expedition leaders decided that the best thing to do was to let Jamie and his buddy team leave earlier than the rest of us the next day, to give them a head start. Bryan looked deeply concerned.

Day two on the mountain dawned clear and bright. It had been a chilly night, and our sleeping bags were heavy with dewy condensation. Coffee revived us though, and I felt my spirits surge as we set out from the camp that morning.

On this second day, we were walking through a landscape that became more and more arid as we went along. The jungle was behind us, and we now ascended more steeply among rocks and through scrub. Some segments of the trail would start off extremely steep, only to temporarily descend into a little valley and turn and go back up even more steeply. This was frustrating to some of our climbers, and understandably so.

Ultimately, though, going up and down in life is frustrating, too—it is the nature of every human experience.

Despite the toughness of the second day, our spirits were still high. We all seemed to share a sense of purpose. At one point, I stood on a bluff and looked back at a long line of climbers strung along the harsh landscape. What immense pride I felt! Among those climbers were people whom society had summarily written off—individuals who in various ways had been isolated or rejected by society at large. But here they were. Who would describe anyone who had the courage to climb Kilimanjaro as "disabled"? Certainly not me.

I watched Gordon at last setting up the big camera on a tripod. He was capturing the vast expanse of the foothills of Mount Kilimanjaro below. Finally, the officials in Dar es Salaam had given us the approval to film with the big cameras. The timing couldn't have been better. The vistas were growing more and more idyllic to film as we climbed. And now I knew that we would capture it all in our documentary.

The views were what compensated for the barrenness surrounding us. As I looked around and focused on my steps and those of my fellow climbers, my spirits soared once more. I remembered the Rose Glow and the way it had beckoned to me years before. My experiences in London over the past few months and the surrounding difficulties were fading into the distance. Here, now, I was breathing in pure, clear air and setting one foot in front of the other in a community of those I cared about. That is what life is about. I was exhausted again—and hungry—when I arrived at the lunch spot, where the tables were groaning with food for us. No celebrity chef had ever prepared better-tasting food, I thought, completely in awe of what our cooks could put together on the slopes of the mountain. We had plenty of fresh fruit, carbohydrates, and protein. It made me appreciate the fare even more when I remembered that every egg, slice of bread, or piece of fruit had been carried by a porter. Again, I felt so glad that I had not cut corners.

As I finished and rose from the table, I suddenly realized that Bryan Magee hadn't sat down to eat with us. He was standing on the edge of the rocky platform, staring back down the trail. His mouth was set into a thin, grim line. I looked around at the climbers shouldering their packs for the next section of trail. There was Michael, but where was Jamie? There was no sign of Pauline, either. Two-thirds of the buddy team was gone. In spite of their early start, they must still be struggling up the trail behind us.

By this point, we'd climbed several thousand feet from the beginning of the trail. We'd already seen and passed the 12,000-foot mark. Yet we were four days from the summit. As the afternoon wore on, some of my exhilaration began to evaporate. I could tell from the faces of the team members that they were feeling similarly. My legs were aching, and my calves and thighs cramped with the repetitious plod upward. The air felt thinner. Every action seemed more of an effort. My head felt so heavy. I paused to take a long swig of water—we had to carry every drop of water with us; there is no drinking water on Kilimanjaro. Dehydration was an ever-present danger, as was mountain sickness. We all had been advised to watch for the telltale symptoms of headache and nausea. If it was ignored, a headache could become dizziness, disorientation, and cerebral swelling. Once that set in, the climber had to leave the mountain and head down—quickly.

The first case of mountain sickness hit without warning that day. Liz had seemed to be doing so well. She was fit and motivated, determined that this trip would change her from a nervous and terrified agoraphobe to a confident, capable woman—a woman who could meet any challenge, even Kilimanjaro. From the outset, she was positive that she would succeed. But this second day began badly for her. She complained of a nagging heaviness and a sensation of pressure behind her eyes. Attributing it to a bad night's sleep in the cold, she kept going. But as the day progressed and she climbed higher, her headache worsened.

The medics examined Liz and pursed their lips. After a while, they determined that Liz had an advanced case of acute mountain sickness and needed to descend quickly. We watched her lonely figure stumble down the mountainside, accompanied by several of the guides. They disappeared around a bend. Everyone seemed a little subdued after that. This was our first climber to turn back. All the climbers knew very well that not all of us might reach the top, but now it was really happening.

On Wednesday, the third day, the reality of our situation came to a head. It was my own personal low point.

Our tents were set up in a small valley, one that we had to descend into through a steep and treacherous trail. It would have been difficult even by daylight. After a long, exhausting trck through the boulder field, I eventually reached camp long after dark. Aching all over while I headed for supper, I told myself that the worst was over. But doubts loomed, and

I fought back more tears. We'd already sent Liz back. Now it looked as if Val Bradshaw had acute mountain sickness, too, and she'd have to turn back. We would be leaving another climber behind.

Had I been wrong to drive this project forward? Were our critics right that we were attempting to climb the mountain too quickly?

In the darkness that night, I'd lost all sense of who was ahead of me and who was behind me. My fellow climbers were just bobbing torchlights in the pitch-black. I knew that Ali, who'd relieved me of my rucksack, and Ahmed had arrived ahead of me. The two Jameses and Alex had safely arrived, too. But what about Jamie and Pauline? They'd caught up with us before. Where were they now? My heart sank when I heard from Eric Murphy, one of the AAI guides, that they were nowhere near the camp. Pauline could probably manage the descent into the valley, but the medics weren't happy about Jamie even attempting it. Jamie, I learned, was still struggling across the boulder field. John Hauf, our experienced lead guide from AAI, decided to stay with Jamie. They would set up a tent there and spend the night. At least they'd be safe.

With Val now incapacitated by mountain sickness and the ever-cheerful Jamie condemned to a lonely night away from his two buddies and the rest of the group, morale was low. How was I to motivate the team? Keeping them all enthusiastic and determined was crucial because I knew that anything we had experienced up to this point would simply be like a warm-up act. Ahead of us was the place where Hans and I had tried and failed to climb Kilimanjaro a decade before. Tomorrow, we would encounter the grim, bare face of the Barranco Wall.

LEADERSHIP LESSON NO. 13: RHYTHM

If you haven't read the Winnie the Pooh tales since you were a child, you probably have forgotten one of the most insightful comments of that little bear. He said: "Rivers know this: there is no hurry. We shall get there someday."

Of course, with deadlines and goals looming, adults find that there definitely is a hurry. You have your eye on a prize, an opportunity for advancement, or a niche in the market, or you are facing the pressure of completing a project at or under budget: there isn't enough time! You know that "he who hesitates is lost," and you need to move with alacrity and singular focus to achieve your objectives. However, rushing wildly toward your goal or waiting until the last moment before a deadline to crash a project is poor judgment.

The best leaders learn how to pace themselves—not just in the office or for their projects but also in whatever they do, both personally and professionally. We dealt with this concept a bit in Chapter 3 when we discussed dividing your journey into steps, but this lesson takes the idea to the next level. You need to develop a rhythm that suits you and that enables you to use your energy as efficiently as possible. If you don't, you risk sloppiness and the likelihood that you won't meet your goal. At worst, you risk physical and mental exhaustion as well.

At the University of Houston's Bauer College of Business, researchers led by Sara Jansen Perry examined this phenomenon. They took a close look at whether goal-focused leadership leads to exhaustion in company employees and what factors contribute to employees' being able to make their goals without exhaustion. Their determination was that such personality traits as conscientiousness and emotional stability are found in those who manage best under hard deadlines and when facing important goals. Such individuals seem to have a natural knack for goal setting, planning, and time management. In short, to paraphrase Perry, they are able to pace themselves.

This is a quality that does not come naturally to me. I am an alpha female, determined to reach my objectives with excellent results in the least amount of time. My background is a testament to that. When I arrived in the United States as an 18-year-old, I felt that I had "lost" a year while my parents and I emigrated to the United States. I was determined to get my J.D. (juris doctorate) degree before I turned 25. There was no time to lose! So, I started college while I was still finishing high school, finished college in three years with a double major and a minor with honors, and graduated cum laude from law school. To top it all off, I took the bar exam for the State of Michigan *before* I finished law school to make sure I did not lose any more time.

While I relished the achievement, I realized that I was not enjoying the journey. The few times when I "stopped to smell the roses" are indelibly etched in my mind. As I continued at a fast pace, there were poignant reminders that this was not the best way to live. My saving grace during this time and during my investment banking career was the discipline of keeping the Sabbath. During law school, every Friday at sunset I would play the "Hallelujah Chorus" from Handel's *Messiah* and put the books on the shelf until Saturday sunset, when the grind would start all over again.

It took me a while to realize that this "Sabbath rest" had probably saved me from a mental and physical breakdown, kept my marriage strong, and helped me to keep my accomplishments and goals in perspective.

PACE YOURSELF

It's important that you develop a rhythm that suits you and that enables you to use your energy as efficiently as possible. It takes fortitude to keep yourself from the natural urge to just get the task done as quickly as possible at any cost. Make sure you get perspective before you make decisions, and learn to pace yourself. Create moments of rest for yourself and the people around you. Recognize that the best employees are not workaholics, but rather people who are connected to the world, who are connected to their families, and who give back to their communities.

Ronald Rigio of Claremont McKenna College's Kravis Leadership Institute and his colleagues published a fascinating analysis of so-called virtue-based ethical leadership.

Drawing from the ancient texts of Aristotle and St. Thomas Aquinas, they examined the four cardinal virtues: prudence, fortitude, temperance, and justice. These, the writers reported, seemed to be consistent with what managerial experts now call "authentic transformative leadership."

It makes sense. Pacing yourself, not racing to your goal in a slipshod manner, does in fact require prudence. It takes fortitude, or strength, to keep yourself from the natural urge to just get it done as quickly as possible, at any cost.

There's more, though. If you want to lead, it does not serve you well if you are the only one who reaches the goal, and you have taken nobody with you. As a young M&A lawyer in New York, I often worked 18- to 20-hour days. The pressure of billable hours was enormous, and I still remember one of my colleagues who managed to bill 27 hours in a single day. When I asked him how on earth he had achieved such a feat, he assured me that he had been working nonstop while flying from New York to San Francisco, and, because of the three-hour time difference, he had been able to bill 27 hours!

Unfortunately, many law firms and investment banks—the industries that I know best—have created an atmosphere in which people are proud of such lunacy! People in leadership positions who do not pace themselves and do not take time to reflect can cause untold damage to themselves and the people around them. It's important that you cultivate a rhythm that enables you to reach your objectives while enjoying the journey. Also, you may be pleasantly surprised that people will want to follow you.

▶ *In conversation with* ◀
CHRISTIE HEFNER

Christie Hefner, the former chairman and CEO of Playboy Enterprises, rose quickly to the top. Upon graduating from college (a Phi Beta Kappa, no less), she began working for the company her father had built. She was a vice president in fewer than five years, and was appointed CEO just a decade later. Christie left Playboy to focus full-time on her philanthropic cause: the CORE Center in Chicago for people afflicted with HIV and AIDS. A business builder at heart, she has just taken on a new challenge as executive chairman of the new Canyon Ranch Enterprises division.

The art of pacing herself is one that Christie has taken to a new level. I spoke to Christie about this all-important quality. Too many would-be leaders rush to the top in a blitz, rather than trying to achieve their goals at a measured, thoughtful pace. Christie learned this lesson for herself at an early age.

"When I was 29, Playboy Enterprises got into serious financial trouble, and I persuaded my father and the board that I was the person who could lead the effort to turn the company around. I realized that in order to be able to do that, I had to pace myself—it was going to be a marathon, not a sprint. And learning to pace myself became critical to my ability to succeed." For Christie, this process did not happen overnight. "It's certainly true that in the early 1980s, when I was first president, I never took vacation time," she told me. But finally, she realized that the key to her sustaining her early success would be "the balance of time between activities that were energizing and activities that were ener-vating."

Christie shared specific examples of techniques that she has used over the years to pace herself. "One of the things I figured out was that it was not necessary to make all the decisions at the moment when problems were presented to me. And I think that often people's inclination is to feel that they have to be responsive immediately, and not only can that be overwhelming, but frankly, it can lead to some 'not good' decision making. Sometimes time is your best ally, giving you the opportunity to gather more information or more perspective, or just to see how things play out. So one lesson I learned was to really evaluate and challenge myself as to whether or not this decision had to be made at this moment."

Christie is a firm believer in choosing one's activities, space, and people. Critical of the notion of excessive face time at the office, she explained what she perceives as essen-tial to leading for the long haul: "The key to having the en-ergy to sustain leadership over a long period of time is less a function of how much time you spend in the office, and more a function of how much of what you do energizes you versus how much of what you do enervates you. In my case, I didn't have to balance the demands of being a parent. I did have a relationship, and ultimately a marriage and a family, but I found that choosing to spend time on those activities that were a source of energy for me was really important, and that this could very much be work-related in terms of in-tellectual stimulation and a recognition that while it is lonely at the top, you are not alone at the top unless you choose to be. If instead you choose to trust people and surround yourself, both inside and outside of your organization, with people whose advice and counsel you respect, that will make a huge difference in terms of your own ability to have the energy to succeed."

For Christie, pacing becomes much easier if one has a healthy perspective on one's priorities and a strong network. "Having perspective on your situation is critical, and that perspective, by definition, comes from stepping back. So . . . for people who are parents, kids give you perspective; for me, giving back in terms of being involved in things that are charitable and civic gives me perspective in terms of what are the really big issues and the big challenges, as opposed to what might be the crisis of the moment. I also think that perspective comes from friends, and I'm a big believer less in mentoring and more in networking, only because I think that the kind of person who can be helpful to you in one situation may not be the same person who can help you in another situation, so having a broad array of people you can call on—in other words, a network—can be an enormously valuable asset."

She also believes that leadership "isn't just about you; it's about the people you are working with." To that end, she has come to believe that the best employees are not necessarily those who are workaholics: "The best employees are people who are connected to the world, who are connected to their families, who give back to their communities, who have interests outside of work, because they bring all that with them to the office environment. And whether you are making a marketing decision or trying to do strategic planning, that broader, more holistic thinking about the world is very helpful. And in turn, if you treat people that way, they will go the extra mile for you. So, I found that if I was able to say, 'You have a child with a substance abuse problem; that's where you need to be right now,' or even, 'If you have a child who is playing in an important sporting event, you need to be there,' then when I had to say, 'I need you here right now for these extra hours or this extra trip,' people would give back."

We have come a long way in the debate about "work/life balance," a phrase that in my view is unfortunate because it certainly helps to be alive at work, since work is an integral part of life. Christie noted the very healthy development in this area: "I started my career at a time when a lot of these issues of work/life balance were just gender issues, but I was out in the workplace long enough to see them become generational issues. I think that young men today are every bit as interested in striking the right work/life balance as young women are."

Last but not least, her advice is to find activities that you can lose yourself in. "Scuba diving does that for me; skiing does that for me; I used to fly sailplanes; even traveling to different countries does that. We are also good at multitasking, so we have to be careful that we do not always have a part of our brain connected to whatever our work is, and sometimes that disconnection is the most energizing thing we can do."

14

The WALL

10 JULY 2008

ALL I FELT LIKE DOING was crawling into my sleeping bag. However, we had to resolve Jamie's situation before morning. It wasn't just the question of whether Jamie could continue the journey, which now looked doubtful. There was a more fundamental issue to discuss, an issue that could jeopardize everything: the buddy system was not working as we had planned. We called a meeting.

Just before the meeting began, I found that we had other problems to face.

"Herta!" It was Steve Ballantyne. "I've just been speaking to the U.K. on the satellite phone. They asked me what the hell is going on up here," he said. "They want to take down the website."

The Enham website? As I wondered what he could mean, my legs began to tremble. We had prepared a website where relatives, friends, and other interested parties could follow our progress, watch our podcasts, and leave messages. Were the people back in England prepared to take the website off-line?

"According to them," Stephen continued, "the expedition is a wipeout. There's pandemonium. Enham has been inundated with calls from parents claiming that we're endangering the lives of their children. They're clamoring to know why so many people are leaving the mountain." Surely, this was a gross exaggeration. But that was beside the point. The reality was that there was one thing we had not foreseen. We had not anticipated that the climbers would send text messages to their friends and families from the mountain, or even that they would carry personal phones at all. Here they were, though—defeated and exhausted, and texting home to share their disappointment and misery with others. Now uncertainty was spreading beyond the mountain. Enham getting panic-stricken calls from families was a disaster that I had never expected.

At a low point after the day's punishing climb through the boulder field, I was raw and let down. The letter that I'd received from our doctor's colleague criticizing our pace came back to haunt me. Had the doctor called the media, too? I thought I'd managed to quell the negativity among the Enham trustees by addressing them directly. But now I was isolated on the mountainside, and it was impossible for me to influence things in England. We could address the issue with the climbers that were with us on the mountain, but what could I do about the concerns that had surfaced in the United Kingdom?

Maybe there was a way—the website. Maybe I could provide a rousing update and explanation for the site the next morning to assure people that we were safe. I needed to make a public statement of our competence and ability to succeed. This was not just to reassure the friends and families back home but also to motivate the remaining team members. But first, we had to have that meeting regarding Jamie and the apparent failure of our buddy system.

Before I left, I reminded myself of that cold statistic: only 35 percent of climbers on the Machame Trail make it to the top. For the past three days, I'd convinced myself that even though part of our group was physically disabled, we could beat the average with our superior equipment, planning, and strong buddy system. Now it all looked overly optimistic.

The meeting ran long into the night. We talked about everything that had gone wrong, and the discussion was difficult and painful. Bryan Magee was tense and angry about his brother having to spend the night away from the rest of us. Tough decisions had to be made. In the meantime, Val, despite her sickness, had managed to arrive at camp. Could she be allowed to carry on tomorrow? The doctors needed to make that call. I dreaded the looks on the faces of climbers who were told that they could not carry on.

Mountain sickness was something that we'd figured prominently into our plans. Jack reassured me that the pace of the climb was perfectly safe, especially given the number of medics we'd brought. But it was the buddy system we had set up to help disabled climbers get up the mountain that seemed at risk. This was one of our project's structural pillars. In some cases, it was working—superbly, even. But in others, as the case with Jamie showed, it was not working at all. Even though the guides stepped in to help climbers as much as they could, the buddy system was fundamental to the project. When and if it broke down, the entire future of the expedition could break down, too.

We determined that Jamie had clearly reached his physical limits. He could not go on. His buddy, Pauline, tearfully admitted that she couldn't go on either. His other buddy, however, the young and strong Michael, could have continued. However, Michael decided to leave with Pauline, and to begin their descent first thing in the morning. Val would descend also. Her AMS had weakened her too much, but she bravely vowed to return as we hugged her good-bye.

As for Bryan Magee, I felt really sorry for him. He was on this trip primarily because his brother Jamie was one of the disabled climbers. Now Jamie was going back down. I could see that Bryan was torn between wanting to accompany his brother and standing on the mountaintop with his disabled buddy, James Bridges. In the end, that was the deciding factor. Jamie's spirit was robust, even though his body wasn't. But James Bridges still needed Bryan, and Bryan decided to stay.

Pauline was in tears by the end of the meeting. She blamed herself for her failure, but I told her and everyone else that it wasn't a failure. They should all hold their heads high. It wasn't a defeat that they didn't reach the summit, but a victory that they had come so far.

The next morning, the beauty of our surroundings was brilliant and inspiring. The sky was blue, and the views were stellar. We had come this far, I told myself, and we would not give up now. A soldier I met once told me, "Show me a hill, and I'll storm it." That's why I climb mountains. The reward is more than a view. It's the journey. It's the knowledge you gain that, in climbing the mountain, you have achieved something hard-fought and worthwhile. On the mountain, as in business and in life, the choice for me is not binary. Valley or peak? Winner or loser? Victory or defeat? It is much more nuanced than that. However, striving for excellence and aiming for the top, taking as many people with you as possible, is a worthy goal.

Making the choice to win is key to strong leadership. It doesn't mean that we don't make mistakes. It doesn't mean that we don't have setbacks. The question is how we react to them. That is one reason why this mountain, this expedition in particular, had become so important to me. I wanted to show that we all have difficulties in our lives. At the same time, we all have talents and the potential for greatness. From the beginning, I had known full well that not everyone was going to reach the summit. In a collective sense, though, it did not matter. Just setting foot on the mountain and making the effort to reach as high as possible was a superb achievement in its own right.

Despite the gorgeous morning, the mood in camp was downcast. Even a single person having to leave the mountain was a blow to morale, and we had now lost several. It was devastating to look around and realize that some of our friends would not be with us at the peak. I could read in the faces of some of our team members that there was even a question of whether *any* of us would make it at all. Maybe with the notable exception of James Smith, who seemed to have no doubts at all.

The best way to get the message out about the actual state of affairs on the mountain was with a Webcast, which we would be conducting that day. I got ready for it as Kate, one of the film crew, set up her equipment. The Webcast would consist of me speaking directly to the camera, with a stunning panorama of mountain and sky behind me, and the notorious Barranco Wall, too. From where I stood, it towered straight up, darkest gray even in the sun, hard and implacable granite. We would have to tackle that, I knew.

I turned to the camera, knees shaking. This speech felt like the most critical one I'd ever had to make, a state-of-the-nation kind of address. I had to be reassuring, not just to the people at home but to those of us up here, telling them that everything was fine, and that we were physically and emotionally able to do what we had set out to do on this expedition—that nothing had gone awry.

I was surprised at how steady my voice was as I explained to my far-flung audience that all the climbers were fine and that those who had descended would be relaxing at the hotel in Arusha until we returned. Then we would reunite. I explained that we had a tough day ahead of us, and thanked our friends and families for their love and prayers. I encouraged them to keep sending their notes of support. As I concluded and watched Kate turn off the camera, it felt like a success. I had faith that I'd make the summit, that this time I'd be able to challenge the Barranco Wall. Somehow, I had managed to reassure myself about all of this.

The Barranco Wall is a hard rock scramble. Not all of us had to tackle it directly. There is a route that skirts the side of the wall, but it is longer and more physically punishing as a result. Gordon wanted shots of climbers taking on the wall from that higher vantage point, so a small group of climbers went with him. They'd join us on the top of the ridge.

Climbing the wall was exhilarating. With the weather so perfect and clear, we could focus on the challenge itself. Although tears had been shed that morning when Val, Pauline, and Michael left us, the team was now energized once more. Whenever someone got stuck, a hand would reach down or someone would offer a shoulder for support. We all helped one another over the difficult sections. It was the reverse of what had transpired the day before, when the team had been demoralized and fragmented. Today, we were together, physically and emotionally, for one another. We were a team! The buddy system again worked the way I had envisioned it.

As we reached the top rim of the wall, the others who had taken the longer, more roundabout route joined us. My heart lifted at last. We had beaten the obstacle that I had worried most about, the one that had stood in my way to the peak a decade before. Standing there at the top of the rim, I knew it. In two days' time, we could be standing on the summit of Kilimanjaro.

LEADERSHIP LESSON NO. 14: OVERCOMING OBSTACLES

Let's take a moment here to define exactly what I mean by an encumbrance or obstacle. It could be any event, habit, person, or behavior that impedes your steady progress.

The near meltdown of the financial system resulting in the recent global financial crisis has become the most challenging event for business executives all over the world.

The very fundamentals of capitalism are being examined and questioned. We are at a critical juncture, and we need to make some tough choices if we want to restore faith in an economic system that has been a significant engine for prosperity for centuries. One thing is for certain: it cannot be business as usual. If we shrug off the crisis and resume our old habits, capitalism will fail us, and with alternative economic systems, we will fare even worse.

What does this have to do with obstacles and removing the barriers that hinder us from achieving success? Everything! This is the time to take a hard look at the habits, cultural conditioning, industry practices, and systems that caused this near meltdown, remove those that are wrong, modify the ones that are outdated or ineffectual, and replace the faulty ones with others that will result in long-term sustainable growth.

REMOVE YOUR ENCUMBRANCES

Apathy and a lack of passion are serious encumbrances that need to be jettisoned and replaced by a positive attitude and a commitment to excellence. Resist short-term thinking and rebuff the tyranny of quarterly results. Train yourself to think globally, not locally, and eliminate people from your life who drag you down.

First, if you want to succeed in this new paradigm, you have to start with a thorough appraisal of your attitude toward your work. Do you have a sense of ownership and a deep level of engagement? A recent Gallup Poll studied employee engagement and reached some stunning conclusions. According to the 2009 poll, only about a third of workers reported that they were "engaged" in their work. A full 67 percent of those polled said that they felt either not engaged or entirely disengaged. Essentially, according to the poll, these employees have mentally and emotionally checked out. Theorists from Harvard University have examined this phenomenon and largely concluded that such employees have lost their passion. Apathy and a lack of passion are serious encumbrances that need to be jettisoned and replaced by a positive attitude and a commitment to excellence. You will not be able to motivate your team and the people you need to win over if you are to meet your objectives if you are not passionate about what you do.

Second, you need to resist short-term thinking. According to Dominic Barton of McKinsey & Company, Asian business executives typically think about their organizations in terms of at least a 10- to 15-year time horizon, while Americans and Europeans tend to be near-term-oriented. This nearsightedness is causing us to invest on the basis of quarterly earnings, to take as much profit for ourselves in the shortest time possible without evaluating the consequences in a few years' time, let alone for following generations.

After my investment banking career, I founded Ariya Capital to do my part in creating a sustainable private equity industry in frontier markets, with my initial focus being on Africa. I firmly believe that a world in which more than four billion people live at or below the poverty line is a smoldering volcano that can erupt when we least expect it. So I kept asking the question: what are the consumer-led growth industries that are at the core of poverty alleviation? Moreover, how can we invest our clients' money to generate superior medium-term financial returns and achieve quantifiable social and environmental benefits? In order to start the firm, I had to examine and set aside traditional views about risk, profit, and results. When I shared my vision with a board member of a major bank, he commented cynically: "It is hard enough to make money the old-fashioned way, let alone worry about that social and environmental stuff." (He used slightly stronger language.) This line of thinking, in my view, is outdated and presents a barrier to future sustainable growth. Fight the urge to think myopically, and take a page out of Warren Buffett's book. According to Buffett, the ideal holding period for his equity stakes is "forever."

Third, think globally, not locally. The bureaucracy or politics that is inherent in most organizations can sap your energy. I am not advocating that you ignore these local issues, but rather that you not make them your focal points. Work around them, where possible, and channel your energy toward outcomes that make you a better citizen of the world. One of the people I hope to hire in the near future is a young African with an MBA from Harvard Business School who has lived in various countries and has decided to go back to his home country and use his skills to help rebuild it. He is already multilingual, but, given China's enormous importance as the increasingly predominant trading partner for the continent, he is learning Mandarin Chinese.

Finally, eliminate people from your life who drag you down. You owe it to yourself and to the rest of your team.

Once you have decided that certain employees need to leave your organization, you should sever your ties with them as compassionately as you can, but sever them you must; if you do not, you will keep the entire team from achieving its potential. This is an ugly part of business, and I am not particularly good at it. However, learning to remove people for the benefit of your organization is essential to realizing your vision.

The singer Jimmy Buffett once noted that "One of the inescapable encumbrances of leading an interesting life is that there have to be moments when you almost lose it." It's an excellent point. When you are dealing with an obstacle that is suddenly thrown in your path, you may feel anger or despair. That is human. But what is not okay is to accept the encumbrance as a fait accompli and lose your passion and momentum.

▶ *In conversation with* ◀
ABEYYA AL-QATAMI

Abeyya is the sixth of eight daughters who were born to Ahmed Abdulaziz Al-Qatami, a Kuwaiti and the first international property owner and developer in Dubai. Today, the Al-Qatami family is one of the ruling families of Kuwait and is among the most influential merchant families in the Gulf region. The family has a strong hold over numerous industries across the Gulf countries.

Abeyya is a former chair of Seven Seas Investment Corporation and sits on the board of IFA Hotels and Resorts, a global luxury chain of hotels. She and her sister were the first women to sit on boards in Kuwait, and she was the first registered female bond dealer in the Gulf. I spoke to Abeyya about overcoming obstacles, and she immediately began by giving me an idea of what her father faced "when Dubai was nothing but a sand dune." He looked at it, she told me, and immediately had a vision that "this land will be a gold mine."

Abeyya continued: "He befriended a young man called Rashid, who was sitting at the port and just looking out to sea. He turned out to be the son of the emir. The two became firm friends and would visit each other regularly." Abeyya's wealthy father was moved by the poverty in Dubai, so he "convinced the Kuwait government to donate schools and hospitals." In 1962, he set up a contracting and property development office in Dubai and started buying up huge tracts of land and persuading his wealthy Kuwaiti friends to invest in Dubai.

"When Rashid's father died, Rashid took over as the emir of Dubai, and my father created the big real estate boom. He got all his friends to buy into the vision—he had so much goodwill that they all followed," Abeyya told me.

Though Abeyya's father was devoted to his daughters, he didn't raise them in the lap of luxury. In fact, during Iraq's invasion of Kuwait in the early 1990s, the family went into exile and flirted with poverty, and also danger. "When Iraq invaded Kuwait in 1990, my parents were in Paris on holiday, so I had to take my sisters and nieces and escape in a jeep driven by a Bedouin, 17 hours across the desert to Saudi Arabia," she recounted. "Only six cars were allowed across the border, and ours was one of them. My spirituality got me through. I kept reciting some lines from the Koran asking to 'blind the eyes of others' so that we couldn't be seen. Miraculously, two Iraqi tanks drove straight past us, but the soldiers, who were armed with Kalashnikovs, were looking the other way and literally didn't see us. If they had, we would have been shot. I had seen them firing on others!"

Abeyya's faith and will, multiplied by the powerful example of her father, got her through that trial and the hardships that followed. She and her family escaped from Kuwait and found refuge in various parts of Europe.

"In exile in France, my father was supporting 30 family members. All our bank accounts had been frozen. We were penniless. We ate only a light meal once a day, and we didn't know when we would be able to get money. This went on for two months," she said. "During this time, I was the only person with a job (I was working for the Commercial Bank of Kuwait in London), and I split my salary with my younger sister."

Even when the family's fortunes were restored after the first Gulf War, Abeyya's father continued to impart a sense of strength and self-reliance. He wouldn't pay for his daughters' education, insisting instead that they win scholarships on their own academic merit.

"When I won a scholarship to the American University in Beirut to study communications, he didn't give me handouts; I had to eat sandwiches like everyone else . . . always scrounging for change," she told me. "And when I went for my first job, my father knew the chairman but refused to help. I had to enter a competition and win a traineeship on my own merit.

"I worked my way up in International Financial Advisors on my own merit. I was already a senior manager when my brother-in-law Jassim Al-Bashar joined to run the company. When he took over, I offered my resignation because I didn't want to be seen as being there because of him, but he said, 'Stay—everyone tells me you are indispensable; I need you.' We were a good double act and grew the company together. Our relationship at work was very formal; we spoke officially to each other and were very businesslike. He was harder on me than on others, expecting more."

Abeyya's high-profile job in the Middle East was something that she had to handle with great delicacy. "My biggest obstacle has been being a woman in a man's world. I always had to be on time, so as not to be called lazy. I had to do more work than anyone else, had to be properly dressed and groomed. I was always the only woman in a group of men, either financiers or engineers. I always had to behave very carefully." This, she explained, was because it is against the cultural norm in the Middle East for a single woman to travel without a family member.

She spoke of the embarrassment of traveling with a married man who turned out to be an alcoholic (drinking is taboo in the Muslim culture). She had to wake him up for meetings. She couldn't shame his family by making people aware of his problem, so she had to handle things very delicately. At the same time, she had to preserve her reputation.

"It wasn't easy. I knew his family, his wife; he could have said anything against me," she said, explaining that removing encumbrances was a matter of always being watchful and careful for them. "Looking back on it, I behaved too much—I didn't even wear perfume, as I didn't want people to say what was that lovely fragrance and draw attention to the fact that I was a woman."

"The financial world is full of temptation—the only thing that kept me going was that I would ask for God's help. There are lots of temptations for women in a man's world. There are lots of tricks we can play, and if you don't play them, everyone is trying to trip you up because they think you are too good to be true."

Abeyya's father was the main cornerstone for her success. "My father encouraged my career and allowed me to travel alone with male colleagues; otherwise my international career would not have been possible," she said, adding that because he was such a peaceful, powerful, and kind man, she never would have thought of shaming him.

"I also had a very strong faith, and my spiritual side kept me strong, so that when people whispered behind my back and gave me funny looks, it didn't bother me.

Flexibility, Abeyya told me, was a main tool in removing encumbrances. "I was taught to be very flexible—to do anything, no problem, on any income, whether ten dollars or a million dollars," she said. That and self-discipline served her well. "My spiritual relationship with God helps me stand up for my principles and what I believe in, regardless of what anyone thinks. . . . My only real obstacle is between myself and God—there is a continuous war with the self, like a wild horse that needs taming. Once you learn to tame yourself, regardless of whatever comes, life gets easier, and temptation falls away."

A recent encumbrance facing Abeyya has been her physical health. After 27 years of working, she began exhibiting symptoms of burnout, with deteriorating eyesight and a danger of heart disease looming. "I had neglected my body. It was time to leave my job, regain my health, and find myself." It takes a keen eye to spot obstacles and to painstakingly remove them, a quality that Abeyya has repeatedly displayed during her illustrious career.

15

ALMOST THERE

NO SOONER HAD WE conquered the Barranco Wall than the weather began to cloud in. This can be terrifying on Kilimanjaro. The rain and mist had made Hans and me turn back the last time we had attempted this mountain. The dark shadows were forbidding, but the clouds lifted after an hour or two.

We now had to follow a tricky path into the Karanga Valley, which was where we would camp for the night. We needed to get a good long rest to build up our strength for a relatively short fifth day that would steeply take us up to High Camp, the last stop before the summit. We would get only a few hours of sleep there before the long final leg of our journey.

As I descended into the valley, I was satisfied about sticking to my choices. They'd proved to be correct. I was glad that we'd used John from AAI as a guide for the climb—he knew the mountain in all its moods. Not only did he understand the mountain, but he understood people. He knew what he could realistically ask us to achieve. A strong advocate of the buddy system, he saw how critical it was to the climb—especially after those shaky hours on day three.

So yes, I allowed myself a bit of self-congratulation at the planning. On a mountain like Kilimanjaro, however, something else plays a role too. Some might call it luck. I thanked God that we had made it this far. Two more days were all we needed, two more days of good weather and two more days of faith.

We'd planned each day's climb to give us the maximum chance of physically acclimatizing to the increasingly thin air at higher altitudes. After the Karanga Valley, which took us downward after rising so high on the Barranco Wall, we faced a punishing ascent. Our destination was High Camp at 4,700 meters. This was quite a steep climb compared with the distance that we had traversed on previous days. After that, there would be just one long night's push to the summit.

I hoped that I would get lucky and avoid the kind of altitude issues that had forced Liz and Val to go back. But by Friday afternoon, I had a splitting headache long before we even reached the camp.

"Maybe we should just go as far as High Camp and stay there," Hans said to me, seeing me suffer. "The others can go on without us."

"No!" I barked. Sick as I felt, I was determined not to fail this time. In my mind's eye, I could see myself standing on that mountaintop, in what would appear from afar as the Rose Glow. Also, by this point in our relationship, Hans knew how to push my buttons—when he allowed me the possibility of giving up, he knew that my determination would only increase.

Hans and I were among the first to reach High Camp that afternoon. It was bitter cold, and the need to work up some warmth had made me stride it out on the trail. But once I arrived, I almost collapsed. My head felt as if it was going to explode. Dr. Jack Kreindler pumped me full of paracetamol and ibuprofen, but he looked seriously concerned. He didn't tell me then, but I found out later that at that point, he thought that my chances of making it up the mountain (or, more precisely, the chances that he'd allow me to) were only 50-50.

I wasn't the only one who was suffering. Morgan, our tall and fit Australian buddy to James Smith, the autistic climber, was also in bad shape. James had two buddies (the other was Claire), but the real bond that had been formed was between Morgan and James. They were always climbing together. From the beginning, I'd worried about James, with his slender build and geeky glasses. I'd wondered if he had the strength to make it to the summit. Paradoxically, his autism actually seemed to be to his advantage—he had a single-minded focus and purpose that some of the more able-bodied people lacked. Now it was Morgan, not James, who looked unlikely to reach the top. Like me, he was suffering from an intense headache and nausea. He'd even told James that afternoon that he was sorry, but he didn't think he could continue.

"Well," said James, "I'm going to make it to the top."

James's determination was so fierce that Morgan felt that he couldn't let his buddy down. In spite of his crippling headache, he packed rucksacks for both of them to climb later that night. Supper was to be early. As we filled our plates, our leader, John, laid it all on the line.

"Everyone will be awakened at 11 tonight. We must be ready to leave by midnight. Anyone who is not ready to climb at 10 minutes past midnight will be left behind."

I knew that we had to make an early start if we were to get it to the summit safely and descend again in daylight, but this military precision seemed excessive. I asked John why we were leaving so early.

It wasn't about the timing, he said: "It's about state of mind. Experience has shown that anyone who can't get his act together by a specific time is never going to make it to the top." John smiled ruefully. "It's my job as leader to be sure that the people who climb with us to the top are capable of making it. So this is my test. Whoever is ready by ten past, goes up!"

That was John's skill as a leader—he was firm but never heavy-handed. By midnight, after grabbing just a few hours of sleep, every single one of us was ready to go.

It was a beautiful night, crisp and clear. The moon shone brightly in a huge, starry sky. There was something utterly primeval about that sky, with its stars blazing, undimmed by light pollution. I felt so privileged to be there at that moment with all these people.

At ten past, we set off as planned, walking slowly, with our torches shining. We all were bundled up against the cold in every piece of mountain clothing we had. We all carried heavy backpacks because we each had to carry our own water supply. The biggest concern at this point was that our water would freeze, so we had insulated it as best we could. In our pockets were packets of sugar-free lozenges. We sucked on them constantly to keep our mouths and throats moist. It was dark, but this time that just added to the excitement as we began this final climb to the summit.

"If you just put one foot in front of the other," John told us, "that will get you there. That's all it takes. It is all about rhythm, about motion, about keeping going no matter what. Don't climb in fits and starts—don't concern yourself with speed. There will be people who pass us, but we will pass them again. We will go slowly, but we will keep going. That way, you conserve all the energy you can."

And this was how we climbed, slowly and steadily. My favorite Tanzanian guide, Elloy, climbed with Hans and me. I had told him one night in camp how this mountain had defeated me before. He just looked me straight in the eye: "Madam, I will do everything in my power to get you to the top." I felt comforted by the fact that he was climbing so close to us now.

If anyone could help me reach the summit, it would be Elloy. It was important to me to feel comfortable around those who knew the terrain best, and those climbers who'd built close partnerships with the Tanzanian guides were having the more enjoyable experiences. Now that Elloy and I were on a first-name basis, I was beginning to understand more about his way of life and the things he worried about. He told me that the glaciers on the top of Kilimanjaro were melting now because of climate change. He wondered whether the rest of the world knew how important that was. Not only did it mean the loss of one of the most beautiful landscapes on Earth, but it also stood as a symbol of how no place on Earth could escape the damage that humankind was wreaking on the planet.

Such conversations only reinforced my determination. Our expedition and the documentary that we were creating about it would be at least a small contribution to public awareness. We needed to help alert people as to what was happening to this extraordinary place.

For hours, we climbed steadily, relying on our head torches for light, careful not to stray from the trail. It was narrow now and bounded by steep cliffs. My legs began aching again as the predawn chill cut through my clothes. I kept trying to remind myself why this was all so important to me, a lifetime ago.

Our first goal was to reach Stella Point by sunrise. If we managed that, we would have an excellent chance of reaching the summit in plenty of time to descend safely in daylight. Although climbing upward in the dark, by torchlight, was easy, descending in the dark is extremely dangerous. It is too easy to stumble and fall, sometimes even fatally.

The trail seemed harder and harder to manage as we went on. Behind us, Alex and his buddy, Luke, were climbing together. Alex was always grumbling, and it seemed to me, in my tired state, that Luke was pushing Alex up half the time. Their amiable bickering reminded me of an old married couple. It was halfhearted, and over time it grew as meaningless as a background refrain. I was losing all sense of time.

"How much longer?" I began asking fairly regularly of John and anyone else who would pay me attention. John wouldn't answer. The euphoria was gone now. I was freezing. When we stopped to drink, I found that my water was frozen solid. So was Hans's water.

"Here," said Hans, unbuckling his backpack. "I have another coat. Put this on." He wrapped me up in a giant fleecy jacket that I had no idea he was carrying. It came to my knees. I must have looked ridiculous, but I did not care. The gesture warmed me as much as the coat.

"Drink," said Elloy, who suddenly popped out of the darkness. He pressed a cup into my hands, and it was blissfully warm, too. It was a miracle that Elloy could conjure up a mug of hot water seemingly out of nowhere on the mountainside. Perhaps he had a Thermos tucked away. Joy shot through me—intense, unspeakable joy. Such a simple thing—a cup of hot water—and tears of gratitude filled my eyes.

"We're going to make it," Elloy said. "You're doing so well. And we're going to make it on time. Trust me. We'll be at Stella Point by sunrise."

Finally, the words I was waiting for: on time! I like punctuality. Maybe it is my German heritage. Elloy must have instinctively known how to motivate me by mentioning being on time. Clearly he knew something about leadership, too.

Over the next two hours, the temptation to turn around and head back down was overwhelming. Put one foot in front of the other, I told myself, echoing John's earlier advice. That's all it takes. Break it down into small components; keep moving; keep going. I tried repeating one of my favorite Old Testament verses: "They that wait upon the Lord shall renew their strength, they shall mount up on wings like eagles, they shall run and not be weary, they shall walk and not faint." That's it, I thought. I don't need to run. Just walk. Walk. John was right, I knew. Helping the team and myself to achieve this goal meant slow and steady progress.

It was extraordinary. We reached Stella Point just as the sun lifted above the horizon. That red, incandescent ball warmed our faces in the freezing air in a way that I will never forget. There are colors in a sunrise that defy description, and so did my feelings at that moment as I experienced the dawn of hope that every sunrise brings. Although the sky must have been gradually lightening for a while, it felt as if we had walked straight out of darkness into this orb of warmth and light.

"Herta, that sun has saved my life." It was James Bridges, whose lean, worn face was suffused with joy. He'd reached Stella Point just ahead of us.

I knew exactly what he meant.

LEADERSHIP LESSON NO. 15: LEADING A WINNING TEAM

Once you have selected your team, it is up to you to create an atmosphere that enables it to win. Differences in personalities, infighting, lack of trust and respect, exhaustion, and countless other eventualities can weaken even the strongest teams.

I love watching Formula One racing, because to me this sport is the ultimate team effort. While the media focus tends to be on the driver, there is so much more to winning the race than the very talented man at the wheel. Looking behind the scenes, one has to marvel at the sophistication of the engineers and the cutting-edge work of the technical team, where even the smallest detail is analyzed and improved. The fact that nothing is left to chance is evidenced by the seamless flurry of the team during pit stops.

KEEP YOUR WINNING TEAM STRONG

Organizational research has increasingly shown that co-ordinating diverse team members so that individuals are able to act from their strengths is key to managing winning teams. Foster the vision of your organization daily, and model it in all the decisions that you make. Value the contribution of each team member. Drive home the fact that there is amazing power in the team, that together you will succeed. Err on the side of overcommunication. Give your team members the necessary space to replenish their emotional, intellectual, spiritual, and physical reservoirs, and encourage shared leadership.

So how do you keep your team in fighting shape? As in Formula One, winning teams have the following key ingredients: mutual respect; a winning attitude; complementary skills, with each team member knowing his role; egos subordinated to the vision; a healthy, sustainable rhythm; a propensity toward overcommunication (rather than under-communication); 360-degree feedback; and trust. As a leader, you need to ensure that these key ingredients are preserved and enhanced. While a lot more could be written about this topic, here are just five suggestions.

First, value the contribution of each team member. In investment banking, it always bothered me that a lot more value was attributed to the front office than to the back office. People in the front office tend to be paid a lot more for creating the profit, while the people in the vital risk management, accounting, legal, and regulatory departments are treated as necessary but burdensome and deserving of much lower remuneration than their front-office counterparts. Having been on both sides, I know that the back-office functions are vital and that keeping the profits through proper risk management is just as important as making them in the first place. This jaundiced attitude toward what functions are important is partially to blame for the current financial crisis. Financial institutions that had strong corporate governance, transparent accounting and management information systems, balanced risk management, and a strong capital base fared a lot better than their counterparts that were lacking in these areas.

Second, communicate, communicate, communicate. Your team members need to know that although their functions may be different, all of them are necessary and mutually reinforcing. Regular feedback on what is going right and what is going wrong along the path to the goal keeps team members focused. Actively discourage backbiting and the formation of cliques. Instead, ensure healthy, transparent communication from the bottom up, the top down, and horizontally. If your team is broken into warring factions, it will no longer remain a winning team. Make sure that you study the personalities of your team members and that you find the right words and actions to encourage and motivate them, both individually and as a team.

While I was pushing to reach the summit of Mount Kilimanjaro and climbing in the darkness toward Stella Point, I desperately needed someone to quantify the journey for me: "How much longer?" Once I knew that we were on time, it made all the difference.

Third, give your team members the necessary space to replenish their emotional, intellectual, spiritual, and physical reservoirs. If any one of these reservoirs is running on empty for any team member, that team member will suffer, and her performance will be suboptimal. The notion that you leave your personal interests, desires, and relationships at the front door of your office building is antiquated. It is up to you as a leader to create an environment in which your team members do not feel that they need to suppress who they are and what satisfies them. While one should control one's emotions, suppressing basic needs is dysfunctional. How many women in the workforce have been encouraged to lie about the fact that their child was sick and needed to be taken to the doctor? How many fathers have missed their daughter's ballet night or their son's winning tennis game because they could not get away from the office? You can ensure that your team stays strong by allowing its members to be authentic at the office and to be transparent about their needs.

As of this writing, I am supported by an incredibly capable personal assistant who has been working with me for more than five years. The mother of a 10-year-old daughter, she has chosen to work from home. Last year her husband was diagnosed with cancer and has undergone extensive chemo and radiation treatments. Throughout her husband's serious illness, she has performed brilliantly. She knows that she is valued and that she can pull back if necessary. And I know that, while she will take time out to accompany her husband to the hospital, she will work late into the night if necessary to ensure that nothing falls through the cracks.

Fourth, encourage shared leadership. Your team must be constantly reminded that its shared wins and losses are felt by all. To avoid apathy, collective decision-making processes are an important part of keeping a strong team excellent. That way, everyone shares the responsibility for outcomes, and the team can act as a unit and react as needed.

Researchers who have delved deeply into this notion of shared leadership almost always note that the winning team must be a diverse one, as I discussed in my earlier lesson on selecting the winning team. Organizational research has increasingly shown that coordinating diverse team members so that individuals are able to act from their strengths is key to managing winning teams. Drive home the fact that there is amazing power in the team, that together you will succeed.

Finally, create "sunshine moments." Celebrate wins (even small wins) for the whole team, even if just one individual is responsible. After all, the whole team is only as strong as the sum of its parts. After completing a major deal, we generally organized a closing dinner for my team and the clients. These were often elaborate affairs, well attended and enjoyed by all. However, the real reason why everyone in the office wanted us to close deals was the fact that my husband would send a large basket of the most delicious baked goods or boxes of chocolates every time we completed a major transaction.

As the leader, you can create the momentum and a shared sense of achievement. Former Chrysler chair Lee Iacocca was right when he said, "I've always found that the speed of the boss is the speed of the team." You are the one who is setting the tone.

The great anthropologist Margaret Mead said, "Never doubt that a small group of thoughtful, committed people can change the world. Indeed, it is the only thing that ever has."

▶ *In conversation with* ◀
THE HON. AL GORE AND DAVID BLOOD

Former vice president Al Gore does not need an introduction. His stellar political career is well documented, and his work in the climate change arena has become known in some of the remotest parts of the earth. Incidentally, our guide Elloy and I discussed the merits of the film *An Inconvenient Truth* when we were close to Uhuru Peak on Mount Kilimanjaro. However, what is not as well known is Al Gore's successful partnership with David Blood and five other partners, who founded Generation Asset Management. Created in 2004, this London-based investment management firm focuses on equity research with a special leaning toward good corporate governance, social and environmental responsibility, and other sustainability factors. The firm is a platform for advocating "sustainable capitalism," a view that both leaders support and have widely written about. "Just the very existence of the firm," said one of my former investment banking colleagues, "reminds us all that there is a better way to do business."

David Blood, a former Goldman Sachs partner, has been a trusted mentor of mine as I have embarked on this third phase of professional endeavor. We know each other well, and rather than talk about "Blood and Gore," I will mostly refer to them by their first names.

I spoke with these two luminaries who, based on their combined careers, could address this subject with almost unmatched experience and authority.

Sustaining the team, Al Gore and David Blood told me, is job one in such an organization. Shared vision, Al said, "is an essential element of a highly functioning team." That means, he said, "reinforcing the vision because it is not sufficient to rely on osmosis for the transmission of vision and values." Even day-to-day decisions, whether they are made at the leadership or the team level, must be on message and perfectly synchronized with the mission, values, and goals that have been set forth. "When we make decisions on a daily basis, it reinforces the vision and values that motivated the journey in the first place."

Both leaders underscored how important it is to maintain team strength by realizing team members' goals and recognizing the lives they live as individuals outside of work. They also recognize the value of bringing it all together.

"We noticed that in our prior lives, people sort of lived in silos. You had your personal life, and you had your job. You had your beliefs, and then you had your philanthropic interest," said David. "So we thought, well, why can't we bring it all together? We're trying to create a culture in an organization that is a bit different. We note that folks—particularly young people—are changing how they think about their work and what is important to them and how they want to be perceived by their peers when they're asked, 'Well, where do you work?' If you're proud to say, 'I work here and here's what we do,' then the probability of keeping those folks is just higher."

Trust, Al added, "is the glue that makes it possible to develop and maintain a shared vision, with shared goals and shared priorities. If it is a vision that feels worth people's best efforts, that just unlocks energy within all the team members. That in itself establishes a powerful momentum toward that shared set of outcomes." What unlocks the energy, he pointed out, "is a moral core . . . it gives us the feeling that our work together is really more important than what any of us working as individuals could seek to do."

Fostering the vision daily and modeling it in all decisions from the leader and outward "gives the feeling that something larger is at stake," Al said. This is also the best antidote for that old chestnut: an oversized ego. "It lessens the role of ego. That's such an essential part of human nature, but often it is an obstacle to cohesion and shared effort, values and goals."

Keeping with the alpine theme, Al added, "I have a close friend near Seattle who has climbed Everest twice and some other peaks. He said the form with which you climb is just as important as reaching the summit." This is another key element in keeping the team strong: encourage the journey, the process, the way you reach your goal to be something that you can be proud of.

This is particularly true when you need to make tough decisions. David said, "I work very hard to understand the strengths and weaknesses of our team and to coach all our team members to help them maximize their strengths and address their weaknesses, and occasionally to make the difficult decisions that we don't have the right person in the chair. . . . You must accept that we expect excellence in everything that we do, and that includes me. I can be fired; I'm the senior partner of this firm and I actually provided the capital for the firm, but I can be fired and should be fired if I don't do a good job. . . . The thing I like doing the least is giving a difficult review or ultimately suggesting that somebody . . . should do something different . . . but it's the right thing to do. It's the right thing to do for the individual, and if you are asking someone to leave, you must do it compassionately, you must do it empathetically, you must ensure that you're thinking about the person's family and that you're helping that person make the transition to whatever the next steps are. But you must do it. You must do it for the individual and you must do it for your team, because if you ultimately allow mediocrity, the team suffers, and your vision becomes obscured." Excellence and fairness must guide your actions.

For David, the key ingredients of a strong team are "hard work and a true passion around teamwork, and . . . core values. These are the three key ingredients, but the fourth would be a view that it ultimately doesn't matter who gets the credit." That is such an important point! I asked David how he deals with superstars; do you single them out? He was very quick to respond, "If you do that, then you don't have a team anymore; so they can be superstars and they may be perceived as such; but with their teammates, they must respect and must encourage and must acknowledge that their success is due to the whole. If you have a series of superstars who don't work together and don't understand how the organization is how it functions, then you're not going to be successful, particularly in times of strife, in times of challenge, or in times of poor performance."

Although Generation Asset Management has gone from strength to strength, increasing its assets under management and delivering steady returns to its clients even during the recent economic downturn, David believes that the firm still has to prove its mettle, because the team has not really gone through a deep crisis together. It seems to me, though, that this "house" is built on a fairly solid foundation.

16

REACHING
the
SUMMIT

12 JULY 2008

FINALLY, AS THE DAY DAWNED, we could see where we were headed and where we'd been heading all along: Uhuru Peak, the summit of Kilimanjaro, at 5,895 meters (19,345 feet) above sea level.

The wonderful thing was that my headache and all other signs of altitude sickness had vanished entirely. We were very high now, and of course breathing required an effort, but it seemed that yesterday's problems had evaporated once we left High Camp at midnight. I was not even dizzy anymore. Thin as the air was, I could breathe without pain.

There was real joy in every step, for every step took us nearer to a visible goal. On the way to Stella Point, we had lost some of the team in the discouragement of darkness. But all the climbers who had made it to the point were eager to make the summit. I watched the surprisingly capable

James Bridges, marveling at how amazing his achievement would be. Because of his spinal injury, James had never left Britain before; he'd never even been on an airplane. Alex and Luke, who'd arrived after us, showed what they could accomplish together. Also, frail James Smith was there, too, with Morgan, even though they had lost their other buddy, Claire. She had declined to remain part of the team, having given up before dawn.

I'd always known that many of the people on the team wouldn't reach the summit. But I hadn't expected the Saudi climbers, Ahmed and Ali, to give up just before Stella Point. Despite Ahmed's cerebral palsy, both were extremely physically fit. Ahmed also had the additional motivation of wanting to climb the mountain in honor of his recently deceased father. But Ahmed had just suddenly sat down on a boulder and announced that he could not go any further. Ali, who felt that he could easily make it to the top, selflessly gave up his chance and descended with his buddy. Ahmed spoke no English, and the guides spoke no Arabic. I felt very sorry for them both. They so nearly made it.

All of these departures from our team had left only three of the original seven disabled climbers who had attempted to ascend the mountain. I monitored all of the remaining members closely. Kilimanjaro has subtle ways of testing the mettle of those who attempt it. In the final stretch, success on the mountain has little to do with strength or fitness and everything to do with teamwork and sheer determination. People who had insisted on climbing individually and broken with the buddy system had largely failed. In Hans, I had the very best buddy, and both of us felt that we could not have made it without our guide, Elloy. Neither could the others have made it alone.

The sun was shining brightly, and we all put on our dark sunglasses. The glaciers were gleaming, and we could see Uhuru Peak in close proximity. However, we were walking at a snail's pace, and each step became more laborious as the altitude increased, as our lungs yearned for all the oxygen we could inhale. It would be another hour and a half before we would reach the summit.

And then we made it! I could hardly believe it was happening, but we were really standing on Uhuru Peak—mission accomplished! The sensation of looking all around us, with 360-degree visibility on a perfect day, was like standing on the rooftop of the world. There was incredible clarity that day. We could even see the curvature of the Earth, something I thought was possible only from space. With the sun shining and the clouds below us, we drank in our success for 30 glorious minutes. Some of us started to cry. We hugged one another and rejoiced each time another of our group reached the peak. Eventually we unfurled an Enham banner that we'd carried all the way up, and took pictures.

Despite my exhaustion, I could have danced with sheer joy. As I turned round again to take in the view, however, I noticed that Hans was literally reeling. I began to laugh—he looked as if he were drunk, staggering around. Then I sobered up quickly. This wasn't high spirits; Hans had altitude sickness—a bad attack, from the looks of it. And he wasn't the only one suffering. I noticed that two of the cameramen had fallen asleep while they were still filming, another symptom of the condition. Out of context, it looked funny, but it was anything but. We needed to wake them up and get everyone down fast.

We had always known that we would not be able to spend much time at the top of Kilimanjaro. Uhuru Peak is nearly 6,000 meters above sea level. At such a high altitude, there is 50 percent less oxygen than there is at the foot of the mountain. The rule of thumb, to avoid the worst effects of mountain sickness, is to ascend no more than 500 meters a day. In our last run to the summit, we had exceeded that guideline. It was a careful assessment that we had made ahead of time. We had climbed to High Camp the day before to give us an extra 300 meters. But now we were going to have to descend rapidly from the peak. Even after knowing that we could anticipate mountain sickness, the speed of its onset was alarming, especially after the euphoria of our arrival on top.

Reluctantly we left the peak and beat a hasty descent. The sun shone powerfully now, which was yet another reason to leave right away. (Not everyone had remembered sunblock.) Altitude sickness takes different forms in different people. It isn't always easy to spot the symptoms and realize that you're succumbing. Some of us had headaches. Others were sleepy. As for my own well-mannered husband, he seemed to take on a different personality and had no sense of balance whatsoever. He tried to sit down on a boulder, but instead landed three feet away. He acted like a drunk, and a surly one at that. When Elloy, who could diagnose altitude sickness, flicked his fingers in front of Hans's face and asked, "Do you know my name?" Hans barked, "Yeah, so what?" Thank God, this agitation lasted for only a fleeting moment.

We were on our feet for 18 hours that day we climbed to Uhuru Peak and down again. We made our way quickly to where the tents were pitched. Everyone was exhausted, but elated. There was no energy left for a celebration that night, though. We stumbled into camp as the sun sank toward the horizon and fell into our sleeping bags. John was encouraging us to make an early start the next morning, so that we could make further progress down the mountain fast. The path that had taken us five long and often painful days to ascend would require only a day and a half to descend.

So on Sunday afternoon, we limped off the mountain and back through the trail gate. All of the team members who had descended earlier came out to meet us. A band of African musicians was playing, and, tired as we were and as crazy as it sounds, everyone began to dance. Despite the disappointment of those who had not made it to the top, there was a tremendous sense of unity and joint achievement. Those who hadn't reached the summit understood that they, too, were a part of our success. We could not have done it without them. Further demonstrating our commitment to unity, before we'd left, each of us had written a brief expression of his dreams, wishes, or desires on a pillowcase, and that pillowcase had traveled all the way to the top with us and down again. Several of the climbers unfurled it in front of the cameras. The dreams had made it to the top, even if not all the writers had.

As we celebrated at the gate, I couldn't help think about the old saying: failure is an orphan, but success has many fathers.

At the dinner to celebrate our achievement, there were happy faces everywhere. James Bridges seemed to have washed his hair especially for the occasion. Here was a man who had seemed like a loner. But he wasn't hovering at the edges anymore. Now he seemed perfectly at ease among friends, at the very head of our celebration. As I turned to get a drink, he stopped me. "Herta, I'm not good with words," he said, "but I just want to thank you. I wouldn't ever have done this without you."

Could I have done it without him and the others? I had climbed Kilimanjaro at a time of personal career crisis, working at a company whose troubles I didn't fully understand at the time. Climbing Kilimanjaro gave me new confidence in myself and my ability to lead under difficult circumstances. Statistically, ours was a hugely successful climb. Compared with the average Machame Trail success rate of 35 percent, almost 60 percent of our team made it to the top. In fact, 16 of our initial team of 28 climbers had reached the summit, including three of our physically disabled members, James Smith, James Bridges, and Alex Adams. They had conquered their own personal mountains up there, as had I.

We had achieved more than we had set out to achieve. Together we had conquered Kilimanjaro.

LEADERSHIP LESSON NO. 16: DON'T STAY AT THE TOP TOO LONG

Altitude sickness, as I mentioned before, takes different forms in different people, and it is not always easy to spot the symptoms and realize that you are succumbing. For example, my very polite husband seemed to take on a different personality and had no sense of balance, some people have headaches, and others simply fall asleep.

Our experience with altitude sickness serves as an apt metaphor for what can happen in business, in politics, and even in philanthropic organizations. The world is full of people who stay too long in positions of power; at best, they tarnish their legacy, and at worst, they can cause untold damage to themselves, their organizations, or their countries.

In business, the financial services sector has recently experienced a meltdown. Many of the firms where I once worked have found themselves in difficulty. I sometimes joke that I had the perfect résumé until September 2008: Citibank, JPMorgan, and AIG. The banking industry is full of examples of those who made their way to the top and stayed too long, drunk on the exhilaration of being there. The temptation is to imagine that it is worth staying for that one last, special deal, to crown a glittering career. But for some, it proved to be one deal too many. Ignoring any criticism that they were becoming acquisitions junkies, or any suggestion that they might be paying more than was reasonable for their target companies, they wanted to be the architect of the biggest deal on the block. Instead of bowing out with their honest reputations intact, a number of these captains of industry have become the most vilified men in business.

While I worked at AIG, then one of the largest and most successful financial institutions in the world, the CEO was Hank Greenberg, a brilliant man who had built the business up from nothing. He was approaching the age of 80, yet he still could not bear to go down from the mountain-top. AIG was his creation, and he refused to talk about reasonable succession plans. Instead of encouraging another good leader to take his place, any individuals who appeared to be nudging toward his lofty position (including his own sons) were swiftly cut down.

Today the mighty AIG has been humbled, another casualty of the global financial crisis, and although Hank Greenberg left the company before the crisis, in my view, his leadership created an atmosphere that encouraged others to ignore the warning signs and take on risks that the company could not afford. Egocentric, macho leaders in pursuit of their own vision may drive a business to the top. But they cannot keep it there without the support of strong teams, of people who speak their minds and hold their leaders accountable. Some people imagine that being humble and willing to listen to others' advice equates to being a doormat, but they are wrong. Humility is not thinking less of yourself; it is thinking about yourself less.

The atmosphere at the top can result in a very jaundiced view of reality. When the chiefs of the Big Three automotive companies in America went to Washington to plead with Congress for taxpayers' money to save their companies, they flew separately in private jets. It simply had not occurred to them what kind of a picture that presented to the people in whose faces they were thrusting their begging bowls.

In our celebrity-obsessed culture, too many people confuse prominence with significance. As one wit said, your

DON'T STAY AT THE TOP TOO LONG

Leave while you are at the top of your game and go back to the drawing board. Create new goals. Start again. Days are long, as they say, but life is short. If you have come this far, there is no telling how much passion and drive you can bring to other endeavors that draw you. But whatever you do, don't stay at the top too long.

nose may be prominent, but you do not actually need it to live your life, helpful as it is. Unfortunately, it is easy to become hooked on prominence. Many people allow their identity to be wrapped up in their business card, and when they are forcibly ejected from their position (pushed from the top of the mountain, as it were, because of their refusal to leave voluntarily), they feel that they have lost what defined them.

What can Kilimanjaro teach us about handling success and failure? My own career began in the legal profession, where success is often measured in terms of how long it takes to make partner in a major law firm. For young people who had worked their socks off first to make it to the top of their class in law school and then to find a job at a prestigious firm, and after that had put in punishing hours to prove their worth, it could be devastating to be passed over for promotion to partnership. As for those who linger at the top too long, what are they doing but constantly depriving others of the chance to ascend their own career mountains? And in the process, they get complacent.

As in business, so in politics. There are plenty of examples of leaders who may have begun by doing fine work for their country, but who have stayed at the top far too long: Mugabe in Zimbabwe and Museveni in Uganda, to name but two. Leaders who stay at the top too long can start to become self-absorbed and delusional. They can make the fatal error of believing their own press clippings and stop listening to critics. Lack of oxygen—of healthy debate, you might say—starts to shut down parts of a once-fine brain.

At the time of this writing, we are living through history in the making in the Middle East and North Africa, where people have become tired of politicians who have stayed at the trough far too long, enriching themselves and their cronies, while a large percentage of the population is deprived of basic needs. Ben Ali of Tunisia and Hosni Mubarak of Egypt were forced to step down from their countries' highest political office after 23 years and 31 years in power, respectively. The Jasmine Revolution sparked in Tunisia will continue to sweep across the region and will result in more casualties among leaders who have abused their power and have completely lost sight of the people whom they should have served.

The wise leader recognizes when it is time to go down the mountain and make room for others on the peak. Ultimately, obsession with success and staying at the top are as dangerous as a lack of oxygen.

▶ *In conversation with* ◀
DR. MOHAMED "MO" IBRAHIM

Mohamed "Mo" Ibrahim is best known as the founder of Celtel, now one of Africa's largest mobile phone operators. The son of a Sudanese clerk, he went from humble beginnings to presiding over the creation of one of the most successful African companies. This was a new development on a continent where business success can usually be traced to "connections" in high places, rather than merit alone.

After he sold Celtel to a Middle Eastern group, he set up his own foundation, the Mo Ibrahim Foundation, to foster improved governance in African countries. The foundation is committed to supporting superior African leadership that will improve the economic and social prospects of the people of Africa.

Best known for awarding the largest prize in the world, the foundation focuses its attention on those who have demonstrated excellence in African leadership. Past recipients include Nelson Mandela, who has been hailed as "the greatest and most courageous leader of our generation"; Festus Gontebanye Mogae, who served as the third president of Botswana from 1998 to 2008; and Joaquim Alberto Chissano, who served as the second head of state of Mozambique from November 1986 to February 2005. He was elected president in October 1994 in the country's first multiparty election, and then again in December 1999. He stepped down from the presidency in 2004 without seeking the third term that the constitution allowed.

Recognizing that it is dangerous at the top, Mo Ibrahim has become one of the strongest promoters of term limits for public office. Mo very clearly explained to me why he is so concerned: "Term limits are very, very important. They allow fresh ideas, . . . fresh people to govern. Anybody who stays too long at the top, even if he was a saint in the beginning, is going to be corrupted. Power corrupts. Suppose that for 20 years, people keep telling you that you are the sun of this country, you are the moon of this country, you are the source of all wisdom—and every single person in the government is someone you appointed. Everybody owes you. After 10 years, you're going to believe all this, believe the stories, start to believe you're invincible."

This view is shared by President Khama of Botswana. When I asked him whether the destructive egos are the result of people just staying too long at the top, he said, "Directly, because this sort of one-man rule that goes on for decades is extremely unhealthy. . . . It would appear that when people come into power, they just totally lose focus. What is the ideal time; how long should someone stay? Initially, when a two-term limit was introduced in Botswana, I was against it, from the point of view that I felt that in a democracy, people should be able to choose their leaders for as long as they think those leaders are doing a good job. So why have a term limit? But then, as time went on, I came to the impression that ten years, which is about two terms, is about the maximum anyone should be in office.

"It's not unique to the continent of Africa. If you look around the world, you'll find that many politicians who are not restricted to two terms would always try to go beyond the two terms. Then their ratings toward the seventh, eighth, ninth year are in decline. And you say what is it that you think you can offer, for another five years, that you are not able to do now?"

Tony Blair made a similar statement at the end of his term when he said, "The best way to deal with power is to relinquish it."

Clinging to power can be fatal in the corporate world as well, said Dr. Ibrahim. "Unfortunately, what we have discovered recently is that we went to sleep, and corporate governance was as bad as public, if not worse, because the public governance in the developed world seems to be working." His comments about the failure of the boards of the major banks revealed how disappointed he was with them. "All these boards," he said. "Grand people are paid millions of dollars to sit on these banks' boards. Where was their oversight; what have they done?"

How can we ensure that we have only boards that will ask the tough questions and really challenge a CEO or chairman who has been there too long? When I put the question to Mo Ibrahim, he said, "Without shareholder activists, I don't see how that will be effected; without really exposing what's happening in each company and the performance of various CEOs, it will be difficult to do that."

The personal mountain that many an accomplished leader should climb, he added, is "vanity." Look around, and "you'll easily see that the people whom we really admire, who have achieved, who have done things, are really humble people who overcame vanity and egos." The danger of being at the top too long, he said, lies in being surrounded by yes-people, by not listening for the truth and listening only to the praise and to people who are "glorifying you."

"I always tell people: try to put yourself in the other person's shoes and see what the other person sees. You cannot be completely absorbed in yourself all the time; you really need views from every side and angle. A good leader is a person who is not afraid to say, 'I don't know.' How many leaders do you see around you who can say, 'I don't know'? They think they know everything, and that is the problem."

Having the courage to admit that you don't know and the ability to seek views from others is a mile-high view that excellent leaders must learn to adopt. Ask your people for input and listen to them. Through his work, Dr. Ibrahim reminds us: never stop learning, and continue to expand your horizons by making room for other people at the top.

EPILOGUE

It is not the mountain we conquer but ourselves.
—SIR EDMUND HILLARY

WE ALL HAVE OUR OWN mountains to climb. That was the mantra we chose for the Enham Kilimanjaro Challenge. It's a simple statement of fact: no matter how much we try to avoid the difficulties in our lives, no matter how much effort we exert to protect our children from pain, every human faces mountains of his own.

Given this reality, I wanted to demonstrate, through a beautiful visual record, two important ideas: one, that we are all entitled to our dreams, and two, that we can achieve more together than any one of us could achieve separately. The film *The Mountain Within*, coproduced by Hans and me, remains to me a profound and heartwarming record of both these truths.

The climbers who chose to see Mount Kilimanjaro as an opportunity to grow and stretch had a life-changing experience. Regardless of whether the climbers reached the summit with us or not, the fact that they even embarked on this opportunity says so much about their character. Pauline, for example, used her setback as a stepping-stone for success. Even though she was unable to reach the summit the first time, she vowed to try again, and she did in fact return to Tanzania in March 2009. This time, she conquered the mountain.

As for James Smith, he has not stopped talking about his experience, and he has since decided, for the first time in his life, to book a holiday for himself. Ahmed complained of sore feet for days after the climb, but in January 2009 he was the star at a major disability conference in Jeddah, Saudi Arabia. In front of five health ministers from different countries, he talked about his African experience and said for all to hear: "I feel like a real person. The foreigners gave me a voice."

I have also changed direction. Now I focus my business experience on making sustainable investments in frontier markets, including sub-Saharan Africa. I believe that a world in which almost four billion people live on two dollars a day or less is not sustainable. To that end, I have decided to invest in growth industries that break the cycle of poverty and have a positive climate development impact.

None of us who participated in the Kilimanjaro Challenge has simply shaken the mountain dust from his or her boots and remained the same. The experience made an indelible impression on each of us, and now we try to aim a little bit higher and reach a little bit further, not as solitary figures but, ideally, as part of strong teams in which each member generously gives and graciously receives.

For me, standing on top of Uhuru Peak was the fulfillment of a 13-year dream. Had I stood there alone, it would still have been an achievement, but reaching the top with my husband and with these wonderful people whom I had come to admire and respect made the experience unforgettable.

Will I climb Mount Kilimanjaro again? I am not sure, as any attempt now would seem anticlimactic. Will I have other "mountains" to climb? Absolutely!

At the time of this writing, not only is the world dealing with the aftermath of a major economic crisis, but we are witnessing the fall of one North African dictatorship after another. It's a chaotic moment in history, not unlike the fall of the Berlin Wall in 1989 and the domino effect that this event created. People all over are becoming more courageous, the barrier of fear is breaking down, and leaders are being held accountable. The lessons in this book are more poignant than ever.

But we are right to question what we have created and what we have lost. We are right to question our business and political leaders and hold them accountable. But we also need to step up to the plate and fill the void with positive forces. We need to face the mountains outside, and also those within.

What are those mountains that are inside us all? I have had some of my most inspiring conversations with the leaders featured in this book. They all spoke of some mountain that they needed to conquer or one that they had already conquered: vanity, excessive love of self, insecurity, fear of failure, and perfectionism, to name a few. But without fail, each one of them still wants to make a further difference, not just to achieve success but to live a meaningful life, where we "learn, earn, and return," as Marty Wikstrom put

it. A life in which we don't just conquer the mountain—
metaphorical or otherwise—but also conquer ourselves.

I entreat you to join me in becoming one of these leaders
in your family, in your business, in your community, and in
your country. In doing so, you will one day look back at this
time of crisis with the satisfaction that comes from having
courageously conquered the mountains within and without,
and with the assurance that you have fulfilled your purpose
in life.

About the Author

HERTA VON STIEGEL, J.D., is the Founder and CEO of Ariya Capital Group Limited, a fund management firm focusing on sustainable investments in Africa. The firm operates from London, Gaborone, and the Chanel Islands and focuses on three mutually reinforcing sectors: clean energy, financial institutions, and telecommunications.

An international executive with a consistent track record of building profitable structured finance businesses, Herta has held senior positions at Citibank and JP

Morgan. Until 2005, she was Managing Director at AIG Financial Products, the financial services division of American International Group, Inc.

A U.S. tax lawyer by training, Herta practiced law prior to becoming a banker specializing in international taxation and mergers and acquisitions. She holds a Juris Doctor degree from Thomas M. Cooley Law School in Michigan, a Masters of Law degree in Taxation from New York University School of Law, and a Bachelor of Arts from Andrews University. In addition, she completed the Executive Program in Corporate Finance at the London Business School. She is a member of the State Bars of Michigan and New York.

Herta serves on several boards in the corporate and not-for-profit sectors, including Camco International (a publically listed global clean energy developer with significant operations in China, the United States, and Africa) and Opportunity International, a global microfinance organization with multiple financial services subsidiaries.

Herta founded and, until June 2010, chaired the Prince's Trust Women's Leadership Group (www.princestrust.org.uk). She serves on the board of The Committee of 200 (www.c200.org), where she chairs the C200 Foundation, and is a member of the Women's Leadership Board of Harvard University's Kennedy School of Government (www.hkswomensleadeshipboard.org).

A popular and highly sought-after speaker, Herta has been featured on CNBC, Fox, Bloomberg, the BBC, SA FM (South African radio), BBC Radio 4, and various financial print media, including the *Financial Times*.

Born in Transylvania, Herta has lived and worked in numerous developed and emerging markets. She is bilingual in English and German and is fluent in Romanian. She is a citizen of both the United States and the United Kingdom.